Body Brokers

Body Brokers

Inside America's Underground
Trade in Human Remains

Annie Cheney

Broadway Books   New York

BROADWAY

Portions of this book first appeared in *Harper's* magazine.

PRINTED IN THE UNITED STATES OF AMERICA

BROADWAY BOOKS and its logo, a letter B bisected on the diagonal, are trademarks of Random House, Inc.

Visit our Web site at www.broadwaybooks.com.

First Edition

Book design by Fearn Cutler de Vicq

Library of Congress Cataloging-in-Publication Data

Cheney, Annie.
  Body brokers : inside the underground trade in human remains / Annie Cheney.
    p. cm.
  ISBN 0-7679-1733-2 (alk. paper)
    1. Procurement of organs, tissues, etc. 2. Procurement of organs, tissues, etc.—Moral and ethical aspects. I. Title.

RD129.5.C4554 2006
617.9'54—dc22   2005054278

10 9 8 7 6 5 4 3 2 1

For my father, Richard E. Cheney

Wherever the corpse is, there the vultures will gather.

—*Matthew 24:28*

Contents

The Main Characters

Jennifer Bittner
Former receptionist, Pacific Crematorium and Bio-Tech
    Anatomical Inc.
Whistle-blower

Michael Francis Brown
Former owner, Pacific Crematorium, Bio-Tech Anatomical Inc.,
    and California Bio-Science Inc.
Now serving twenty years in a California prison for embezzlement
    and mutilation of human remains.

A. Gray Budelman
Funeral director, Orange, New Jersey
Owner, Mortuary Services of New Jersey

Jim Farrelly (deceased)
Victim, Bio-Tech Anatomical Inc.

Bonny Gonyer
Knee-surgery patient
Recipient of CryoLife tissue

Brian Hutchison
CEO, Regeneration Technologies, Inc.
President, RTI Donor Services

Dr. Gerald Kirby
Former professor of anatomy, Tulane University School of
    Medicine

Brian Lykins (deceased)
Knee-surgery patient
Recipient, CryoLife tissue

Dr. Michael Mastromarino
Former dentist, New Jersey
Owner, Biomedical Tissue Services Ltd. (formerly Biotissue
    Technologies LLC)

Ernest V. Nelson
Body broker, California
Former owner, Empire Anatomical Services
Arrested by UCLA Police Department in March 2004 for receiving
    stolen property.
Free on $30,000 bail.

Joseph Nicelli
Funeral director
Former partner, Biotissue Technologies LLC

Agostino "Augie" Perna
Body broker, New Jersey
Owner, Surgical Body Forms (formerly Limbs & Things), Mobile
    Medical Training Unit (MMTU) and Innovations in Medical
    Education and Training (IMET)
Investor and client, Bio-Tech Anatomical Inc.

Arthur Rathburn
Funeral director, Grosse Pointe, Michigan
Former diener, University of Michigan Medical School
Owner, International Biological, Inc.

Dan Redmond
Inspector, Crematories and Cemeteries
California Department of Consumer Affairs

Henry Reid
Embalmer, Los Angeles, California
Diener, UCLA School of Medicine
Arrested on charges of grand theft, March 2004.
Free on $20,000 bail.

Charley Reynolds (deceased)
Body donor, Tulane University School of Medicine

Rene Rodriguez
Homicide detective, Riverside County, California

James E. Rogers
Founder, ScienceCare Anatomical, Inc.

Richard Santore
"Crazy Eddie of the Funeral Business"
Former funeral director, Brooklyn, New York
Founder, Anatomic Gift Bank of New York

John Vincent Scalia
Funeral director and body broker, Staten Island, New York
Owner, National Anatomical Service, Inc.

Daniel Schonberger
Driver, Pacific Crematorium

John Schultz
Roller hockey coach
Former partner, California Bio-Science Inc.

Dr. Leonard Seelig
Chairman, Department of Cellular Biology and Anatomy,
    Louisiana State University Health Sciences Center, Shreveport

Louie Terrazas
Crematorium operator, Pacific Crematorium, Bio-Tech
    Anatomical, Inc.

Allen Tyler (deceased)
Diener, University of Texas Medical Branch
Consultant, Surgical Body Forms
Employee and partner, Bio-Tech Anatomical, Inc.

Jim Walsh
FBI agent, Texas City

Joyce Zamazanuk
Mother of Jim Farrelly

Human Price List *

Head	$550–$900
Head w/o brain	$500–$900
Brain	$500–$600
Shoulder	$375–$650 (each)
Torso	$1,200–$3,000
Forearm	$350–$850 (each)
Elbow	$350–$850 (each)
Wrist	$350–$850 (each)
Hand	$350–$850 (each)
Leg	$700–$1,000 (each)
Knee	$450–$650 (each)
Foot	$200–$400 (each)
Whole cadaver	$4,000–$5,000
Eviscerated torso	$1,100–1,290
Cervical spine	$835–$1,825
Torso to toe	$3,650–$4,050
Pelvis to toe	$2,100–$2,900
Temporal bones	$370–$550
Misc. organs	$280–$500 (each)

* These prices are valid *only* for fresh/frozen parts that are used for research and education. The prices may vary depending on the source and the broker. Transportation may or may not be included in the cost.

Body Brokers

Introduction

"You are a little soul carrying around a corpse."
—*Epictetus*

One spring weekend in 2003, I attended a medical conference in Miami at the Trump International Sonesta Beach
Resort. The Sonesta is a tower of antiseptic luxury rooms
looming over an otherwise decrepit strip of shuttered motels.
It offers private balconies with built-in Jacuzzis, a full-
service spa, and a $6-million swimming pool "complex" as
well as an enormous ocean-facing conference center booked
with corporate retreats, annual sales meetings, and wedding
receptions. The event that drew me there, organized by a
company called Innovations in Medical Education and
Training (IMET), had taken over the conference center's
Ocean Room, named for its commanding view of the pale,
glassy surf.

For this seminar, the gold taffeta curtains had been drawn
and the room accommodated not a board of directors or
the families of a bride and groom, but rather six stainless-

1

steel gurneys on which rested the legless, armless, headless remains of six men.

Gathered in groups of two or three around each of the torsos were the customers: thirteen urological surgeons from Canada and the United States who had covered their heads in blue paper shower caps and pulled blue surgical gowns over their golf shirts and Dockers. They had come to learn hand-assisted laparoscopic nephrectomy, a new procedure for removing a kidney through a tiny incision in the abdomen.

Laparoscopy demands great skill in operating a fairly specialized set of medical instruments. If the surgeon misjudges the distance between his scalpel and the patient's kidney, he might seriously injure the organ. Most of the surgeons at this conference didn't learn this technique in medical school, so they'd paid up to $2,395 each to IMET to provide them instructors, state-of-the art equipment, fresh cadavers, and a place to practice.

I watched a surgeon adjust his gloves and peer eagerly through his wire-rim glasses at the anonymous flesh. The torso was wrapped tightly, meticulously, in black plastic and secured to the gurney with gray packing tape. The plastic had been peeled back to reveal the corpse's belly, which, owing to the force of gravity, was now a cavernous depression of chocolate-gray flesh.

Next to the torso was a round instrument tray from which the surgeon selected a scalpel. He carved a line through the glistening skin near the navel all the way into the abdominal cavity. Using a smooth plastic ring called a Lap Disc, he stretched the incision into a bracelet-sized opening, through which he inserted a hose that was in turn connected to an air pump. Then he inflated the man's stomach like a balloon. As the torso rose, the skin peeled in places, revealing pale flesh underneath and emitting the faintly sweet smell of decaying bowel.

Beneath this canopy of flesh, the surgeon could now go about his work. He had already successfully performed this surgery twice on live patients. But each time he got close to the big blood vessels, he found his hand shaking. A trip to the Trump resort, with its promise of Florida sunshine, luxury rooms, an oceanfront view, and fresh torsos, seemed like a perfect way to build his confidence.

The surgeon had a partner, who looked sick and pale. Before the lab and after eating a lunch of cold cuts, he had excused himself to take a walk outside. I watched him as he paced around the balcony. "I still haven't gotten over the cadavers from medical school," he said.

Nonetheless, he managed to perform his part in the surgery, which was to insert a long, telescopelike camera into the Lap Disc. Presently, the corpse's interior was revealed on a video monitor above the body. It was a glossy landscape, globules of yellow fat clinging to marbled red tissue. While his partner held the camera, the surgeon made two smaller incisions above the navel into which he inserted two nickel-sized, sharply pointed shafts known as trocars.

Like the Lap Disc, trocars allow surgeons to manipulate

instruments inside them without harming the surrounding flesh. The surgeon removed the camera from the Lap Disc and inserted it into one of the trocars. Then he inserted a Harmonic Scalpel into the other. The Harmonic Scalpel uses ultrasound technology to both cut and coagulate tissue. One of its advantages, according to its manufacturer, is that it creates "minimal smoke."

The scalpel and camera in place, the surgeon rubbed his right hand with lubricant. Then, like a tentative magician, he reached through the Lap Disc into the dark, wet, icy mass of the dead man's torso.

As the other doctors delved into their patients, a New Jersey businessman, Augie Perna, stood watching from the corner, sucking his teeth. Perna is noticeably short, with delicate, pretty features and thick, dark brown hair. He was dressed in his usual business attire: green surgical scrubs, pale blue Puma sneakers, and, hanging on a chain around his neck, the golden head of Jesus, crowned with thorns. Perna is the founder of IMET—"I'm the head cheese," he said by way of introduction.

Although we had never met in person, I had been investigating Perna since 2002. In January of that year, I had received a phone call from an editor at *My Generation* magazine. "We've got an assignment for you," he said. "We want you to write a story about people who donate their bodies to science when they die."

The phone call caught me off guard. Only a month before, I'd learned that one of my good friends from college had committed suicide. The thought of writing about death—just a month after his funeral—was unbearable. I'd hardly eaten or slept, and I was still haunted by the image of my friend—only twenty-eight years old, with a wonderful future—a man who usually wore blue jeans and a T-shirt, dressed in a stiff black suit, lying dead in a coffin. Despite the valiant efforts of the funeral director, he didn't appear peaceful or asleep. His body was wasted, his nose misshapen, and the expression on his face oddly waxy.

But something compelled me to accept the assignment. I think I hoped that writing about body donation would ease my pain, remind me that the dead can help the living. I had no idea then where the story would lead me or what I would uncover.

At first, my research yielded a simple story: Generous people donate their bodies, and in doing so they help to advance science. Cadavers enable medical students to learn human anatomy. They make it possible for scientists to further their research and for companies to develop innovative medical technology. In some cases, dead bodies even save lives. As I reported the story, I visited medical schools. I watched as the students thoughtfully examined each artery and vein and identified the important organs. I spoke to researchers who used cadavers for crash testing cars and to develop protective gear for soldiers in the perils of war.

If I had approached the assignment at another time, I might have focused my attention solely on the uses of corpses, not on the corpses themselves. But losing my friend had emboldened me. Now, I was curious about the dead and also a little protective. I wanted to know everything about them: where they had come from, whom they had belonged to, and how they had ended up in the hands of scientists.

So I started asking specific questions about the corpses: How are corpses acquired? What are the costs? Who is paid? How does a dead body wind up on a crash-testing course? Is it shipped or delivered by truck? Does the family of the deceased know about it?

That's when the story took a turn. Confronted with my questions, many people whom I interviewed, who were otherwise eager to talk, began to stonewall me. To my great confusion, they concluded that I was writing an exposé. They thought my article would discourage people from donating their bodies. Over and over, I had to reassure them that this was not the case.

Their resistance piqued my interest. Just before the story went to press, I made a lucky call to an anatomist at a medical school.

"Who regulates dead bodies?" I asked him.

"Who are you?" he said.

I explained in the gentlest tone I could muster that I was writing for a magazine published by the American Association of Retired Persons. There was a pause. Then the anatomist said, "If you don't mind holding, I'd like to close my door."

When he came back on the line, he said. "You and I need

to talk. Body donation is wonderful. But if you pull back the tablecloth from this wonderful feast, you'll see there's rotten wood underneath."

The anatomist suggested that I write something about surgical-training seminars. He said the courses were often held in hotels—a practice that, amazingly, does not break any state laws—and that they featured human body parts obtained through a little-known and largely unregulated network of independent operators. Human body parts are an industry, he said. "Here's a name. Augie Perna."

So I began to investigate Perna and his industry. I learned from the National Funeral Directors Association that in 2003, 73 percent of American corpses were buried and the rest were cremated. I also learned that no one keeps track of what happens to corpses before they reach those final destinations.

At that moment, I began another story, which was published in *Harper's* magazine and inspired this book. I spent three years investigating the underground trade in corpses and body parts in the United States. Though I focused on body parts used for research and education, a largely unregulated business in the United States, I was shocked by what I found in regulated sectors of the corpse trade, including practices that put patients' lives at risk.

———

Every year in the United States, tens of thousands of corpses enter the cadaver trade, a business that supplies the bodies and body parts of the dead to scientists, surgical

equipment corporations, hospitals, pharmaceutical companies, and researchers all over the world. Corpses that enter
this business are cut up into parts, not unlike chickens, and
distributed through a complex network of suppliers, brokers, and buyers. Some corpses remain whole.

In the cadaver business, suppliers sell bodies and body
parts to brokers, who in turn funnel them to buyers. Suppliers include morgues, medical schools, tissue banks, independent companies, funeral homes, and even, on occasion,
crematoria. Brokers, who facilitate the corpse sales, may
be independent businessmen or employees in some of the
same places. Their clients include medical associations,
major U.S. corporations, researchers, doctors, and hospitals. The demand for bodies and parts surpasses the supply,
which keeps the prices of human flesh and bones very high.
Each corpse that travels through the system can generate
anywhere from $10,000 to $100,000, depending on how it
is used.

Whereas the Uniform Anatomical Gift Act, approved
and recommended for enactment in all states in 1968 and
amended in 1987, prohibits buying and selling dead bodies,
the law allows companies to recover their costs, which
makes life very easy for brokers. By inflating the amount
they spend on labor, transportation, and storage of bodies,
they can easily hide their profits.

With so much money to be made and a limited corpse
supply, players in the cadaver trade are not always scrupu-
lous about the way in which they acquire dead bodies. Most

bodies that enter the cadaver trade are acquired legally, with consent from the deceased person or his or her family. Still, even in the case of legitimate donations, the donors often have little more than a vague notion about how their bodies will be used. Most are never informed that the cadaver may be sold off to middlemen or parceled out to surgical equipment companies. Certainly, none of them imagines that their relative's torso will end up taped to a gurney at a Trump resort.

Some in the cadaver trade employ sinister means to acquire corpses: deception or even outright theft. Bodies headed for cremation are particularly vulnerable. Only ten percent of states in the U.S. inspect crematoria or require their workers to be certified. Roughly half of all states have no laws governing cremation at all. The average untrained crematorium worker earns minimum wage and may be easily tempted by the body parts business. As one crematorium employee pointed out, when it comes to ashes, "There's no way to tell if you're missing you head or your shoulders or your knees."

The trafficking of corpses is nothing new. In fact, the cadaver trade has a long history in the U.S. The business was born in the late 1700s, when surgeons began dissecting cadavers to learn human anatomy. At the time, there was no legal supply of corpses, so surgeons enlisted the help of "resurrectionists" or "ghouls," as body snatchers were known—a class of cagey, often desperate men who trolled the cemeteries of New York and other cities on the East coast, stealing bodies from graves and selling them to doctors and to medical schools. By the mid nineteenth century, the country was teeming with these men. Body snatching was a grim business, but then, just as now, corpses paid handsomely. In 1828 in New York, a ghoul, who would have made a dollar a day as a laborer, could sell a corpse for ten dollars.

The cadaver trade faded during the late nineteenth and early twentieth centuries, as laws were passed around the country designating unclaimed bodies and the bodies of paupers fair game for dissection. But over the last fifty years, science has found new uses for corpses, and the demand for them has once again surpassed the supply.

Today, roughly 10,000 cadavers a year are used to introduce U.S. medical students to the miracles of anatomy. They are also used for postgraduate seminars for surgeons, and for commercial seminars held by instrument companies like Bristol-Myers Squibb, Medtronic, and Johnson & Johnson, which use human body parts to demonstrate the latest medical gadgetry. Fresh corpses also serve as the raw material for research experiments, and in the production of a variety of surgical and cosmetic products. Bones can be ground into dust that is made into paste and used in periodontal surgery; hearts can be dissected, and their valves transplanted into living people; skin can be used to patch the bodies of burn victims, or it can be freeze-dried, stored, rehydrated, and injected into lips, sagging facial lines, and penises; and on and on.

Some corpse applications receive more scrutiny than

others. Though many Americans associate underground corpse trafficking with organs, the federal government actually does a good job regulating organ procurement organizations. By law, organ-procurement organizations (OPOs) must be non-profit charities, which means that their financial records are open to the public. They cannot compete for donors, since only one OPO is allowed per region, and their organ related activities are routinely audited by the federal Department of Health and Human Services. If an OPO isn't meeting its legal obligations, the federal government can shut it down.

The federal government also regulates transplantable tissue, which includes heart valves, bones, veins, corneas, skin, tendons and ligaments. The Food and Drug Administration inspects tissue banks to ensure that the tissue they supply to hospital patients is free of disease.

But the federal government does not regulate bodies and body parts used for research and education. Much of this business takes place in the shadows. If a body broker decides to form a company to sell body parts for research or education, there is no one to check his books or to make sure he obtains bodies legitimately. The federal government does not regulate nontransplant tissue banks. Only New York States licenses them, and until 2004, New York did not regularly inspect them. No agency keeps track of how many bodies go into the nontransplant system and no one knows what happens to them. Bodies and parts may be funneled to or stolen from medical schools, tissue banks, morgues, funeral homes, or crematoria. The buyers receive little more than a package of parts and ID numbers. No one besides the broker or supplier may know where the parts came from or how they were acquired.

The cadaver trade has flourished as Americans have disassociated themselves from death. Most people today see their loved ones for the last time in a casket. Two hundred years ago, families buried their own dead. If a beloved relative died, the women of the family laid out the body at home. They washed the body, and, when they were finished, wrapped it in a cloth and called for the undertaker. The undertaker was in most instances, a local man, perhaps a cabinetmaker earning a few dollars on the side building coffins. In many cases, the undertaker knew the deceased or the deceased's family, so he had a natural respect for their feelings.

Things might have proceeded along these lines, if it hadn't been for embalming. During the Civil War, doctors pioneered the technique of embalming, which involves siphoning blood from a corpse and replacing it with chemicals to preserve the bodies of fallen soldiers so that they could be sent home. After Abraham Lincoln died in 1865, word of this miraculous procedure spread. Lincoln's body was embalmed, then paraded around the country on a funeral train for twenty days. Americans came by the hundreds of thousands to see it, marveling at Lincoln's lifelike appearance.

Undertakers realized the financial potential of this new science and quickly put it to use. For a fee, a corpse could be saved for up to a week with an inoffensive odor. Now the funeral could wait for the distant relatives to arrive. As it was no longer necessary to say a rushed good-bye, it seemed only proper to display the body in an expensive casket and make it the centerpiece of an elaborate funeral.

For the first time, some funeral directors became prosperous men, serving a large area and people they didn't know personally and reinventing undertaking as a profitable business. Now it became more and more common for the people who handled dead bodies to have never known those people or their families in life. More and more often, what was required of a funeral director was feigned grief, a spectacle worthy of its great cost, the illusion that the corpse was in a peaceful sleep.

Today, most Americans wouldn't dream of handling the bodies of their dead friends or relatives alone. Even though most states allow it, almost no one chooses to bathe their dead relatives or to lay them out at home. Families don't prepare corpses for burial or cremation or lay them in the ground themselves—they entrust these things to funeral directors.

As we have grown more distant from death, we have also grown more deferential to doctors and scientists. Body brokers count on this, cloaking their greed in appeals to help the future of science and medicine. "I equate it to a confidence-game swindle," an FBI agent who's investigated body parts thefts told me. "How do you gain the confidence of the guy you're trying to swindle? You bring in the confidence man. This has got a confidence man built into it.

You're dealing with doctors. Who comes to the table with more credibility than doctors? People go, 'Obviously, this is legitimate. There's a doctor involved.' That's the steamroll that makes it happen."

In this book, I focus on the suppliers, brokers, and buyers of bodies used for medical education and research. I write about a crooked crematorium owner, greedy medical school employees, and complicit professors who are lured into the business by brokers offering lucrative deals for body parts. And I write about the brokers themselves, entrepreneurs in the shadows, who make sales to major U.S. corporations in need of body parts. These companies close their eyes to the unethical and sometimes criminal aspects of the cadaver trade, while accepting the anonymous product it offers.

I didn't intend to write about transplantable tissue, which is regulated by the FDA. But I discovered disturbing connections between this business and the underground brokers supplying body parts for research and education. I found a similar culture of secrecy in both fields, especially where profits are concerned. Where I found connections, I wrote about them.

What follows is the story of what I found when I immersed myself in the underground cadaver trade: a macabre world populated by odd, strangely alluring characters. The players in this business have an unusual relationship with death and dead bodies. To them, corpses are commodities like any other, something to be sold, like a television set or a new car.

Over the course of my investigation, I found myself disturbed and sometimes even amused by their unusual take on death. Most of all, I was shocked to learn that American corporations, researchers, and even physicians have been supporting the underground traffic of these brokers for years. The cadaver trade is hidden in plain sight—in our hospitals, in our boardrooms, on our highways, and in our cemeteries. This book is my attempt to reveal it.

chapter 1

Wilderness

Joyce Zamazanuk knew that her son was dying. She knew it when the nurses quietly wheeled Jim to a private room on the seventh floor of the hospital in San Diego. His new room had a bed, a metal chair, and an oxygen tube, but little else. Outside, few visitors wandered the halls. A hush hung over the nursing station. Joyce thought, *This must be where they bring the sick patients to die.*

Six days in the hospital had done little to help Jim. AIDS had ravaged his body. The tumor that engulfed his lungs appeared larger in each new CAT scan. Always slender, Jim Farrelly, forty-five, was now reedlike beneath the cotton sheets and blankets. His thick brown hair had thinned to a soft, downy fur. He had trouble talking. Death by asphyxiation was certain.

Joyce wondered what awaited her beloved son: Would he feel pain in the moment of his passing? How much longer before he left her?

Joyce had been just seventeen years old when Jim, her third son, was born; the two had always been close. Even as a baby, Jim was gentle in his manners and feminine in his tastes. He wanted to do whatever his mother did. Unlike his macho brothers, Jim would learn to cook and to sew. Later, when his sister was born, he styled her hair and embroidered flowers on her clothing. At school, the other children called him all the usual names: sissy and mama's boy.

But Jim was a scrapper, tougher, his mother always said, than any of his tough brothers. When they lost Jim's father, it was Jim who stepped in and took care of Joyce. Jim planned his father's funeral. He bought the Christmas presents. He was a comfort to his mother. When he grew up and settled in San Diego, Joyce often came to stay. She and Jim shared their sorrows and secrets.

AIDS was one secret Jim had tried to keep. When he was diagnosed with HIV in 1994, he lied to his mother and said, "The doctor just found a polyp. Nothing for you to worry about." Joyce was relieved. But within a year, the virus had progressed to full-blown AIDS.

Jim tried to prepare his family for his death. He knew it was coming—he'd seen many of his friends die—and so he made sure everything was ready. With the little money that he had, he bought a cemetery plot in Arizona. He drew up a will and arranged to be cremated through a funeral home in San Diego. With his debts paid and his last wishes clear, Jim assured his mother there was nothing more to worry about.

The end came quickly. Jim had only been on the seventh

floor for six or seven hours when he began making a gut-
tural, gasping sound. By now, everyone had arrived: Jim's
sister, Joy; his best friend, Billy, and countless others. Startled, they rushed to his bed.

"What is it, Jim?" his mother asked.

"Can I help you? You're not crying. Please don't cry."

Jim shook his head. He was laughing. "It's okay, Mom,"
he whispered. "I am less and less. There is more and more."
Then he fell into a coma. Soon after, he was dead.

Everything went as planned. In the hospital room, Joyce
said good-bye to her son. After she went home, the nurses
came and took Jim's body down the long hall, into the
freight elevator, and downstairs to the morgue. Several
weeks later, someone from the mortuary called Joyce to say
that Jim's ashes were ready. "Okay, send them along,"
Joyce replied. But when the urn arrived, she didn't open it.
She clutched it and placed it on her shelf, where she gazed
at it for weeks. Finally, she sent it on to Tucson, where it
was buried beside the urn of Jim's father.

Fourteen months passed. Then, one afternoon, the telephone rang in Joyce's house.

When she answered it, a woman asked, "Are you the
mother of Jim Farrelly?"

"Yes," Joyce said. "What is this regarding?"

"I'm a victim's advocate."

Joyce wondered if one of her sons was playing a joke.
"But my son is dead," she said.

"Yes, I know," the woman said.

Could it be identity theft? Joyce pressed the phone to her ear and took a deep breath. "I don't understand," she said. "What is this about?"

The female caller paused. "I'm calling to tell you that your son has been the victim of a crime."

"A crime?" Joyce almost laughed.

"Ma'am," the woman's voice was somber. "We have identified your son's body parts at a crematorium. His body was dismembered."

Dismembered? But Jim's ashes . . . He'd been buried. He was *fine.* Joyce said, "I'm going to have to call you back."

Later, Joyce would recall that final night in the hospital. In retrospect, it seemed odd to have left Jim alone. And yet, what could she have done? No one had invited her to the morgue. Did the hospital even have one? Joyce had never thought to ask. The nurses, who had been so solicitous when Jim was alive, said nothing about his corpse. Joyce had signed some papers at the funeral home. But she never saw Jim's body. Now, Joyce wondered: Where had they taken him? Why hadn't she been there for her son?

Corpses lead a perilous existence. Whisked from the arms of family and friends, they embark on a journey under the care of strangers. In most cases, those to whom we entrust our dead take care to ensure that they're laid to rest safely. Most morgue workers, funeral directors, and crematorium operators keep careful track of each body. Indeed, many care for them as they would the dead bodies of their own relatives. Still, body brokers have been known to haunt this dark landscape, hunting for body parts, which they can later sell.

At each stage of the journey, there is ample opportunity for theft. At the hospital, a nurse or an attendant shuttles the corpse first to the morgue, where it's stored in a steel refrigerator. If a family requests it, an autopsy may be performed. As it happens, an autopsy is an ideal situation for body brokers inclined to theft. Pathologists routinely take samples of specimens relevant to their investigation—a slice of kidney, for instance—which get preserved in paraffin blocks and transferred onto slides. An honest pathologist may remove a whole brain and keep it fixed in preservative for weeks. Otherwise, the brain matter will not yield its secrets. This is perfectly legal as long as the doctor has permission from the deceased's family.

But consent forms vary in their specificity, and pathologists often work with unlicensed assistants known as *dieners*, a word derived from the German for servant. Dieners do the work that no one else wants to do: They dissect bodies, cutting through bone and muscle and removing whole organs so that the pathologists can weigh and examine them. They are responsible for cleaning up the morgue and assisting pathologists. A diener may work with a pathologist, while at the same time harvesting body parts for tissue banks. Stealing body parts is easy for a diener, and the money is good. Dieners often become brokers.

Numerous diener thefts have been discovered over the years, from Maine to Los Angeles. Nearly all of these cases were uncovered purely by chance. Often the families of the dead noticed something odd on an autopsy report. Only later did they learn that parts of their family member's body had disappeared owing to an intricate deception.

If an autopsy isn't ordered, someone at the hospital calls the funeral home of the family's choice. A driver comes to pick the body up and take it to the funeral home. There, the body is refrigerated until the time comes for what's known in the funeral trade as "final disposition." If the body is to be cremated, it may be sent to another funeral home equipped with a crematorium or to a crematorium at a nearby cemetery. Here, once again, a stranger, who often has little training or supervision, assumes control of the body. If the crematorium operator is so inclined or is familiar with the market, he may be tempted to remove a body part before sliding the cadaver into an oven. Once a body is cremated, there's no way to know if anything is missing.

If the body is to be embalmed, the procedure takes place at a funeral home. But there too, a corpse may not be safe. The funeral home may have an agreement with a tissue bank. Each body may produce a tidy kickback, a thousand dollars, perhaps. Or, more disturbing, the funeral director may own his own tissue bank, earning thousands of dollars selling the parts of each corpse entrusted to his care. He might not bother to ask permission.

Relatives rarely have the opportunity—or the inclination—to accompany their deceased loved ones into the realm of hospital morgues and funeral homes. They sit by their bedsides while they are alive, clutching at any sign of life. But once death comes, they are quick to release them into a world, which, for many, is a kind of wilderness. And there, as in the wild, vultures are drawn to the dead.

chapter 2

An Ideal Situation

In 2001, Michael Brown had a thriving cremation business in Lake Elsinore, California, a pleasant suburban town seventy miles southeast of Los Angeles. He had five admiring employees, a beautiful wife, and two sons. Brown, who was in his early forties, was a loving and supportive father. On most weekends, he could be found racing dirt bikes with his older son and attending the boys' ice hockey games. Brown took both boys camping in the Nevada wilderness. He Jet Skied with them on the town lake, played golf with them, and taught them how to fly radio airplanes. Brown beamed when he spoke of his children. "Those kids are my heart and soul," he said.

Brown wasn't a devout Christian, although he displayed in his spare office a Bible engraved with his name. Sometimes he even quoted Matthew 7:3—"Why do you see the speck that is in your brother's eye, but do not notice the log that is in your own eye?"

The California state crematorium inspector, Dan Redmond, saw this same humble philosophy in Brown's work and was impressed by it. "You can honestly tell when these guys are just in the business to make an extra buck, and Mike was not like that," Redmond said. Redmond noticed that when Brown talked to grieving families, he listened, counseled, and was careful to avoid any sales talk or to push a fancy coffin. If a family couldn't afford a funeral, Brown offered to cut his rates or provide a service free of charge.

"He had one of the best crematorium in southern California," Redmond said with a smile. In 1996, when a nearby funeral home got in trouble for improperly storing bodies, Brown was the first man Redmond called as his expert witness. "When other guys in the business had problems, I used to tell them to go and look at Brown's place. That's how a crematorium ought to be run." Brown's records were always in order; there was never a document out of place, never a signature missing. He was constantly mopping and sweeping.

But beneath his caring manner, Brown had little feeling for his customers, living or dead. Later, he would say, "I don't believe a body is worth more than garbage once you pass away."

———

One afternoon in February 1999, Jennifer Bittner stood in the parking lot of Brown's crematorium. She was a pretty, pale-skinned girl, with delicate features, blue eyes, and long brown hair that she wore loose down her back. Bittner appeared older than her eighteen years. Her shoulders slumped and her face was drawn with grief.

Shading her eyes from the glaring sun, Bittner stared at the long, low building. Made of stucco and stone, the crematorium was like all of the other buildings in the office park. It was flat and rectangular and resembled a warehouse. Bittner couldn't see much through the tinted glass door. But looking up, she could make out three small chimneys.

When Bittner appeared in Michael Brown's doorway, he jumped up, shook her hand, and led her into a back office. Brown made an impression on the young woman. He was about six feet tall, blond and blue-eyed, with the muscular build of a high school football star. Bittner admired his neatly trimmed goatee. Later, she recalled finding him "very attractive." He was also instantly empathetic. Brown listened and patted her arm as she explained that her cousin had just died and her family didn't have enough money for his funeral.

"It was gang violence," Bittner said softly. "My cousin was murdered."

Brown nodded gently and offered to arrange for a discounted funeral. "I'll take care of everything," he promised.

After they made the funeral arrangements, Bittner asked Brown if she could take a look around. She had always been curious about dead bodies. In her spare time, she read Patricia Cornwell mysteries, books like *Postmortem* and *Cause of Death,* and she dreamed about one day investigating crime scenes.

Brown led her to a front room, past a fifty-gallon salt-water fish tank that he had set up in the corner. Inside the tank, an eel slithered among schools of porcupine fish. Bittner followed Brown, past the couches in the company's waiting room, to the crematorium facility itself, where dead bodies in cardboard boxes lay on steel gurneys waiting to be cremated.

"Oh, wow!" Bittner said when she saw the bodies. "This is kind of cool."

"It doesn't bother you?" Brown asked her.

"No," Bittner said.

Sensing her interest, Brown noticed something else about the young woman. She was stoic. Despite Brown's seeming compassion for others, he had little patience for people who freely expressed their emotions. During the short visits that he shared with families, he was able to indulge them their grief and even tears. But inside, he was disdainful of this sort of "drama" as he called it.

A few days later, Bittner stopped by the crematorium again. "She wanted to look at dead bodies," Brown recalled. He offered her a job.

Jennifer Bittner became Brown's fourth employee, joining Daniel Schonberger, Louie Terrazas, and Dave Smith, a funeral director who soon left the company. Smith was the only funeral director on staff. When he quit, he left his funeral director license behind, and it hung in the front office. Schonberger did the pickups and the deliveries. Louie Terrazas ran the ovens.

All four employees drank too much, but this didn't bother Bittner. Their troubles were familiar—a little too much drink, a few too many arguments at home—but, like her, they were all trying to make their way in the world, and she quickly felt like part of the family. Bittner enjoyed Brown most of all.

Every day at five o'clock, after she closed up the office and Terrazas shut down the ovens, Bittner and the others lingered in the downstairs office to talk. As the cool California evening set in, they finished off the day drinking beer. There were days when they would pick up a bottle of tequila or a bottle of gin. Brown would mix a batch of gin and tonics and the four of them would sit around in the office until nine or ten at night, drinking and laughing.

Brown was never in a hurry to get home to his wife and sons. He had an audience at the crematorium. No one nagged him. His employees laughed at his jokes about prissy funeral directors, the ones he called "stiff-necked liars." Once in a while, they talked about the bodies that they cremated. They wondered aloud about the lives of the deceased, like the six-foot-tall black transvestite who was delivered still dressed in a wig.

Bittner was thrilled with her new job. She was happy that everyone liked to stay after work. It felt like a real family, and Brown always included her in their parties.

There was just one thing that bothered her about the job. Too often, when she answered the phone, there was an angry creditor on the other end looking for Brown.

Bittner tired of these unpleasant phone calls, particularly when she realized that Brown never bothered to call the people back.

Still, the phone calls were a minor irritation, and Bittner was growing fond of her boss. One night, after the others had gone, Bittner climbed the wooden flight of stairs to Brown's office, where he was finishing some paperwork.

Brown had been spending a lot of time up in his office, alone. He had always needed time to brood. Now, with some very ambitious plans, he needed more time than ever.

Shortly before hiring Bittner, Brown had received a phone call from a company called IMET—Innovations in Medical Education and Training. A caller had explained that they were looking for a place to store some human torsos for a surgical training course IMET was sponsoring in San Diego. Afterward, they'd need to have the torsos cremated.

"Can you help out?" the caller asked.

"No problem," Brown said.

With its unspoiled beaches and easy access to airports, southern California is a popular place for seminars in medical training of all sorts. Throughout the year, hundreds of surgeons, eager to learn the latest techniques and catch some sun, arrive at conferences held at hotels up and down the coast. Some of these courses need suppliers to produce human body parts and to dispose of them afterward.

Brown was intrigued by the opportunity, especially since he was planning to build a new crematorium across the street. Several funeral directors had already invested in the project. It was going to be three times the size of his current one—with a chapel for more than a hundred people. There would be a ceramic-tiled room overlooking the ovens, where family members could witness the cremations of their loved ones. Body parts could be another source of income.

Brown already knew that a crematorium was an ideal location for a body-parts business. He knew it after reading a true-crime paperback that his brother-in-law had given him called *Ashes*. "I slept and drank that book," Brown later said. The book described the gruesome exploits of a man named David Sconce. During the 1980s, Sconce ran the Lamb Funeral Home in Pasadena, California, with his parents. Sconce's great-grandfather, Charles Lamb, had started the business, and by the time David came along, most anyone who was anyone in Pasadena sent their family members to the mission-style mortuary with the charming turret.

Little did the families know that Sconce had set up a tissue bank in the back room of the funeral home. With the help of his Japanese assistant, Sconce carved up bodies that he was supposed to cremate. He removed their teeth, eyeballs, and hearts, which he later sold for thousands of dollars to a biological-supply company. The families got back the ashes of whatever was left over and never suspected a thing.

Brown thought about the market for body parts and his new crematorium. What if he set up a legitimate company that accepted body donations, just like a medical school?

He could offer his clients a free cremation in exchange for a body donation. He didn't need to get a license or take a class. All he had to do was register the business with the state.

Brown had everything that it took to run a willed-body program: the crematorium and the clientele base. He had just signed a contract with the county to cremate the bodies of the indigent and unclaimed. With all of the bodies coming in, he thought, "it was an ideal situation."

What he needed were some lower-level people with resolve.

Jennifer Bittner had made her way upstairs, past Louie Terrazas's office. She appeared now in Brown's office doorway. Brown laid his eyes on her soft baby flesh, her long, thick hair, her slightly parted lips, and he saw that she was eager. That night, he seduced his young employee. It was his first transgression—Brown was married, after all, and Bittner was just eighteen. Perhaps he hoped that by keeping her close, he would seal the success of his plan.

———————

A few days before the San Diego surgical course in February 1999, the frozen torsos arrived at Brown's crematorium. As he had agreed to do, Brown left them out to defrost in the embalming room. He placed the limbless bodies out on steel gurneys, and within a few hours, the torsos began to "sweat." Droplets gathered like dew on their icy skin and a fetid, watery, pink liquid trickled from their orifices into the gurneys' troughs. Brown poured this bloody water down the drain.

After the torsos had softened up, Brown stored them in the walk-in refrigerator. On the appointed day, he packed them in Styrofoam containers in his van, drove to San Diego, and delivered them to a conference room at the US Grant Hotel.

Intrigued by what he might see that weekend, Brown booked a room. As night fell, he settled himself in the Grant Grill Lounge, a wood-paneled, dimly lit bar by the lobby, where he was soon joined by a tall, soft-spoken man in his fifties, who introduced himself as Allen Tyler, a part-time consultant to IMET.

Brown took in Tyler's houndstooth sports jacket, his crisp pleated slacks, and his penny loafers. Tyler was articulate, almost professorial. He struck many people as a doctor.

But, in fact, Tyler was a diener. For most of his life, he'd worked at the University of Texas Medical Branch in Galveston, overseeing the school's willed-body program. He'd never attended college. He had grown up on the sleepy island of Galveston and, like Brown, had married out of high school. Then he went to work in the medical school morgue.

The two men hit it off. As the lead corpse experts on the job, they toasted each other with a glass of Johnnie Walker Black Label, then spent the evening chatting, drinking, and watching sports on the big-screen television at the bar. They didn't know it yet, but they had a lot in common. Both enjoyed sports and the outdoors. Brown liked camping. Tyler was an avid fisherman. Both men had two sons. Tyler didn't mention his family at all, or how much his life had changed since he had met IMET's founder, Agostino Perna.

Before they said good night in the bar, Tyler and Brown agreed to meet again in the morning. Over the next couple of days, Brown hung around in the conference room, watching the gynecologists as they probed the vaginas of the dead women. When a torso needed adjusting, he noticed, the doctors called on Tyler to help. Tyler gingerly moved the chilly flesh into the right position, raising or lowering it so that the doctors could get a good view. When the dead ladies began to smell, Tyler spritzed them with deodorizer. At the end of the day, he packed them into Igloo coolers. The next morning he brought them out again. Brown looked on in amazement. He couldn't believe his luck. Here he was, owner of the best and soon to be biggest crematorium in southern California in a room full of potential body-parts clients.

The second night, at a formal dinner hosted by IMET, Brown got to meet Agostino "Augie" Perna. "Augie was real quiet, and he thanked me profusely," Brown said. Perna, he noticed, spent his money freely. "Augie was your quintessential jet-setter. He always wore a white T-shirt and cowboy boots, and he always carried $1,000 cash. I knew that if I was to advance in the field, I needed him."

Perna must have recognized something in Brown, too, because nine months later, he called him.

"We need your help," he said. This time Brown was needed in Las Vegas.

Early one morning in November, 1999, Brown and his pickup man, Dan Schonberger, headed north on Interstate 15 through the flat Nevada desert. They were driving a white van full of dismembered women. The torsos had been packed in Styrofoam coolers, two dead women to every box. It was a five-hour drive to Las Vegas from Lake Elsinore. The road was nearly empty, and the two men were on a straight shot through the Mojave. Except for an occasional passing truck, they were alone in the desert. The only sound was the lulling hum of their tires on the asphalt. Brown opened the window to catch a breeze off the mesa. It couldn't have been more than sixty degrees, which was a good thing, since heat speeds decomposition.

Brown rested his left elbow on the window and massaged his goatee as he drove, pondering the weekend. Gynecologists from all over the world were coming to Las Vegas for the annual meeting of the American Association of Gynecologic Laparoscopists. Augie Perna was their point man for torsos. Tyler would be there, too. "Allen took care of the flesh," according to Brown. "The man knew the inside of the human body in unbelievable professional form." This was Brown's chance to sit down with them face-to-face. It wouldn't be a hard sell. Brown was a natural at marketing. "Mike could sell you ice cream in New York in ten-below weather," Louie Terrazas said. He just had to get the pitch right, make them see that they needed him.

Five hours later, just as the desert was beginning to heat up, the van descended into the valley around Las Vegas. Brown was feeling pumped. He blinked and rubbed his chin one last time and tightened his body. As soon as they pulled up in front of Bally's Hotel and Casino, he began instructing the valets, giving orders as if he'd been hauling torsos his whole life. But Perna had already arranged for a guard to take them up to the ballroom with the coolers. Brown had worried that someone might ask questions about the boxes, but no one said a word.

It was a long trip through the hotel, but everything went smoothly. They unloaded the van, wheeled the boxes into the freight elevator, got off on the second floor, carted the boxes through the kitchen—greeting the chefs along the way—and delivered them to the Pacific Ballroom, where Perna and Tyler were waiting under sixteen glittering chandeliers.

Perna had hired a former pig farmer to come out to Bally's and help with the corpses. There were some other husky men hanging around. They moved boxes and set up tables. By late morning, when the gynecologists arrived, the work of these corpse roadies was done.

Later that day, Jennifer Bittner and Louie Terrazas showed up. Bittner had never been to Las Vegas. Everyone assumed she was a doctor, despite her obvious youth. She didn't correct them. She just let her conference badge speak for itself.

Bittner was eager to get out on the strip, to check out all the fancy casinos and see one of the free shows. That night, she spent some time in the bathroom fixing her hair and putting on makeup and a black dress and platform shoes. Then she joined Perna, Tyler, and Brown at the bar. The three men were telling jokes and laughing, and their confidence was infectious. Bittner hopped up on the bar stool next to Brown. She was still only nineteen, but the bartender didn't ask for any identification when Bittner ordered a drink. That's how it was when Brown was by her side. People treated her like a woman.

After a few cocktails, the group split up. Tyler joined Brown and Bittner, and the three of them headed across the street to the Bellagio. The people at this hotel were different, Bittner noticed; they were L.A. types with hair that cost more than her week's rent. She could only imagine what it must cost to stay at the Bellagio.

Brown was thinking about money, too, as he made his way into the hotel and strutted up to the bar with Tyler. All around them, the music of money was playing: the hollow thud of dice on velvet, the plastic tap-tapping of chips.

For the first time, Brown talked about getting into business with Tyler. "It was a dream think-tank," he said. The next day, they talked about it again. They talked about it on the casino floor, in elevators, but mostly in bars. "Give me the ball and let me run with it," Brown said.

———

Tyler, Perna, and Brown made an ideal team. Brown was about to open his new crematorium and had easy access to corpses. At the time, Perna, who specializes in torsos, was getting most of them from Tyler's employer, the University of Texas Medical Branch, which required a lot of paperwork and fees, and often the further hassle of getting the torsos to California, where many of his conferences took place. Perna had the capital and the connections to make it all possible. Tyler, meanwhile, had the expertise that Perna and Brown required. He knew how to cut and sew and clean up the flesh.

Brown wasted no time. Shortly after they got back from Las Vegas, he moved his employees across the street to the new crematorium. One day, he strode into the back room and tapped Louie Terrazas on the shoulder.

"What's up?" Terrazas asked, wiping the sweat from his brow, as he turned from the oven where he was cremating a body.

"Do me a favor. Go to the liquor store and pick up some vodka and beer and stuff to make mixed drinks," Brown said, reaching into his back pocket and handing Louie a $100 bill.

"Why?" Terrazas asked.

"Remember the people we met in Vegas? They're coming over here, and they're going to meet with me today."

Terrazas hopped into his car and did what Brown had asked. Only later did he ask him what was going on.

"I'm going to start something, and we're going to make some money and we're going to pay some bills," Brown replied matter-of-factly.

"What's it going to be?"

"We're going to be disarticulating bodies," he said.

One day, Brown stuck his head into the embalming room, where Bittner was straightening up.

"I'm starting a new company," he told her with a smile. "And I want you to be a part of it."

Bittner had been growing tired of being a receptionist, so she received this bit of news eagerly.

Brown closed the door.

"You may have to work some overtime," he said gently, "but don't worry about it. I'll pay you for it." He moved closer to Bittner now, fixing his sharp blue eyes on her soft face. "The reason I'm telling you this," he said, pausing, "is there may be some gray areas that come up. I want you to know that I'll take care of them. But, if you ever say anything to anybody, I'll take you down with me."

Bittner wasn't listening. She was already lost in thought, contemplating her future: more money, more responsibility, a new life. Maybe she could buy a nice house with a backyard, she thought, or travel.

"Okay," she said, nodding blankly.

By February 2000, the deal was done. Brown secured a $3,000 investment from Perna and incorporated his new company, Bio-Tech Anatomical. Getting started couldn't have been easier. All he needed were a couple of meat freezers and some butcher knives and band saws.

The only thing left to do was to print up brochures. Brown took his time with this. He wanted the pitch to be perfect. Words were important to him. As a kid, he and his siblings used to practice their vocabulary at the dinner table. "Mike was a literature person," one of his employees said.

Indeed, Brown chose his words carefully. "A willed-body gift will not only ensure the continued proliferation of health sciences," he wrote, "but will surely give a chance to those that have lived without sight, sound, or the ability to walk, new opportunities to experience life more fully. Silent teachers, remarkable heroes, a legacy that few could boast."

He dedicated a section of the brochure to the "culture" and "values" of the company. "We are in this business because we want to offer a rational and compassionate alternative to the 'closed-door,' costly, and unsatisfying services put forth by the Funeral Industry," he wrote. "And if we can make a living in the process, that is the kind of incentive we can all accept. And we can hold our heads before God and our neighbors."

Brown christened himself president of the company. Allen Tyler received the title supervisor of anatomy, and Perna was restyled "Dr. Agostino Perna, Ph.D." Perna never even graduated college, but the Ph.D. attached to his name was enough to make him look like the head of an anatomy department at a medical school.

Once he'd taken care of these details, Brown sat down with Tyler to come up with a price list. For heads, they would charge $500; shoulders, $350; elbows, $350; torsos, $600; spines, $1,250; and knees, $400. Altogether, one cadaver would yield $4,450, more than four times what Brown earned from a cremation.

Tyler agreed to fly out to California every other weekend to disarticulate the bodies. Brown paid him $2,500, plus expenses, for each trip. Perna's companies, in turn, got all the body parts they needed.

———

Twelve miles south of Brown's crematorium in Murrieta, Ronald King, sixty-nine years old, had been diagnosed with lung cancer. It would have been hard news for anyone, but King had already lost his beloved wife, Margaret.

King tried his best. In the afternoon, he watched a little television on the couch in his mobile home. He read the local newspaper. At suppertime, he heated up a box of macaroni and cheese in the microwave. Once in a while, when he was feeling particularly lonesome, he put on a Glenn Miller record to remind him of happier times.

Three or four days a week, King's stepson, Mike DiMeglio, stopped by. "Come on," he'd say. "Let's take a little walk and enjoy the weather." But King preferred to stay close to home. The only things that really cheered him were his plants. He'd take his stepson out to the backyard and show off his cactus collection. There were at least fifty of them, in pots of different sizes. They were perfectly kept. King was forever fertilizing them, trimming the old flowers, fussing over the new buds. "This one here's not blooming yet," he'd say. "But this other one's just about to start. It's going to be beautiful."

King once said these things with great enthusiasm, but

now he was just talking to comfort himself. On the morning of May 3, 2000, he stayed inside and lowered the blinds. Then he got out his prized 1918 Winchester pistol. He placed a pillow behind his head. On the table, he left a check for $850. It was exactly enough for his cremation. He also left a note: "I want to be cremated." Then, just like that, Ronald King was dead.

Nine days later, Allen Tyler boarded a plane for California. Tyler was sporting a new look, which had surprised his wife of thirty years. Gone were the penny loafers and dress slacks that he usually wore. "Mr. Conservative is wearing blue jeans!" his daughter teased when she saw him in his new burgundy cowboy boots and jeans. Tyler just smiled and nodded.

It was a beautiful spring weekend in Lake Elsinore. The air was fragrant with the smell of rose blossoms. On the hillsides, even the Mexican sage, which just months before had appeared withered and near death, had burst forth with new purple flowers. Hummingbirds hovered, supping on the delicate sage nectar. The boughs of the Valencia orange trees strained under the weight of their ripening fruit, which would be ready to pick in just a few days. The bees made their rounds among the bougainvillea and the pink hibiscus flowers. All over the parched valley, a rebirth was under way.

Jennifer Bittner awoke feeling cheerful. She knew that Tyler was coming. For the past several months, he'd arrived promptly every other Friday. She looked forward to his visits, when she got to put on doctor scrubs and rubber gloves and hang out in the embalming room. Lately, she'd been dreaming about moving to Texas and becoming Tyler's apprentice. He had been her age when he got his job at the university. *I could follow in his footsteps,* she thought. It would be a step up in her career—the fantasy of working in forensics seemed ever closer—and she'd need the money soon enough.

Bittner, it turns out, was five months pregnant. Her belly was just beginning to show under the blouse she wore to work. But it wasn't Brown's baby. She had a new boyfriend now, a young man named Steven McCarty, who worked construction laying bathroom tiles.

Even with a baby growing inside her, Bittner was unfazed by the corpses around her. In fact, she loved going in on the weekends to help out. "Show me how to cut," she'd say to Tyler. Then she'd watch closely as he maneuvered his steel blade through the yellow fat and pink muscle and along the smooth white bones of his subjects.

The extra money didn't hurt, either. Always generous, Brown now lavished Bittner with cash and gifts. Each weekend that she worked for Bio-Tech, Brown paid her an extra $200. He gave her $3,000 to put a down payment on a car. He paid to have the windows tinted, he gave her money for a stereo system, and every so often he slipped her $300 just to buy new clothes. She said, "There was hardly ever a time when I could ask for money and he would tell me no."

When Tyler and Brown arrived at the crematorium on

Saturday morning, they went into Brown's office and closed the door. Bittner knew to leave them alone. While she waited, she slipped a blue paper gown over her jeans and T-shirt and covered her sneakers with elasticized paper covers. She brushed her long, chestnut hair into a ponytail, making sure that all of the stray hairs were caught in the elastic. She washed her hands and dried them and put on a pair of new powdered rubber gloves. When she was finished, she waited eagerly in the back of the embalming room for Brown and Tyler.

The room was narrow, like a shoe box, with a white linoleum floor polished to a glossy finish. There were two porcelain basins in the back, with hoses attached. Lined up lengthwise in the center stood two stainless-steel gurneys.

Next door, Ronald King lay in the darkness of the walk-in refrigerator on a metal shelf along the wall. He was dressed as he was on any other day—in Levi's, a flannel shirt, and tennis shoes. King had been dead for ten days.

Stacked above and below him were other corpses in various states of decay. Like King, they came packaged in coffin-shaped cardboard boxes used for cremation, and body bags, inside which some of them wore their own clothing—a velvet dress, a pair of old shorts, shoes without socks. Others wore hospital gowns. A few had been dead a long time and were crawling with maggots.

Brown had flagged the choice specimens. Now Ronald King was hauled in and hoisted up on the table, and his cool body slid out of the box. Once King's clothes were removed, Tyler stepped back to survey his subject. He walked around the table, peering at King's feet and hands and head. He pointed out to Bittner the bullet hole in King's cranium.

Then, Tyler snapped a pair of pale rubber gloves over his ebony skin. He straightened out King's limbs and set to work.

Holding a large butcher knife, Tyler positioned the wide, shiny blade at the sternum and began cutting through the fat and muscle around the outside of King's pale shoulder until it detached in one piece. It was striking to Bittner how quickly he could do it, how easily the body came apart if you knew where to cut, piece by piece, flesh separating from flesh as if God had meant it to be taken apart this way.

Even Michael Brown was awestruck. He had seen human bodies in every condition imaginable, "bloated and shot up," but until he met Allen Tyler, he'd never actually gotten inside a human corpse. There was something primitive and barbaric about it that aroused his emotions—the blood splattered about the embalming table, Tyler's wet, sticky gloves. Yet Tyler was so precise, his motions so masterful. It was hypnotizing to watch his slender hands move about the corpse. With each slice of the knife, Ronald King became less recognizable—until, at last, he lay in pieces.

Tyler handed King's shoulders to Bittner, who rinsed off the blood, wrapped them in a plastic bag, and secured the bag with gray masking tape. Then she neatly placed a label on the package of flesh and set it aside. Later, she would take it upstairs to the attic and lay it in one of the meat freezers.

The three of them went on in this way, methodically moving from body to body, part to part. Tyler removed Ronald King's elbows—one slice on the forearm and two swift strokes forward with his saw until the bones snapped in two. Then his hands and his knees. One slice on his calf and his thigh, a few cuts of his saw, and the leg came right off. Then his head. Tyler plucked out King's brain like a smooth boiled egg from its shell.

When Tyler was finished, the only thing remaining on the table was the old man's torso. Bittner hosed the blood off King's pale chest, wrapped the torso, and set it aside with the other parts. Then, in her girlish print, she listed each part on a scrap of paper as Brown had instructed her: *King, K66M—mid tibias, knees, torsos, forearms, elbows, shoulders, head w/out Calveria.*

Over the course of a weekend, Tyler could make it through ten corpses, depending on what he removed— sometimes more if he was feeling energetic. By the time he was finished on Saturday, he had also cut up a sprightly seventy-two-year-old, who had died in the advanced stages of Alzheimer's, and a Navy veteran. Tyler tossed the leftover scraps of flesh into a cardboard box. Then he and Brown went out to eat and have a few beers.

It wasn't until a week or so later that Bittner found time to sit down at her desk and type out the death certificates. She turned on her typewriter, settled herself in her chair, and gathered her papers. Bittner enjoyed this part of her job. Naturally organized, she sorted her files by color: a blue folder was for a body that had been donated to Bio-Tech Anatomical, and a manila folder was for a regular body that was supposed to be cremated. Each time she filled in a death certificate with the name of a deceased person and tucked it away in the right file, she was filled with a sense of satisfaction at knowing that everything was being done just right.

But today something was wrong. Ronald King's folder was missing the consent form required for any body that had been donated to Bio-Tech. By law, King's family had to sign a form giving permission for his body to be used for science. Bittner looked through the papers in King's file again, but all she could find was a request for cremation signed by King's stepson. She checked again, but sure enough, the Bio-Tech consent form was missing.

There must be some mistake, Bittner told herself. But as she looked for the papers, she nervously recalled other cases. When Tyler cut up a body, it had been her job to record the name of the corpse. She didn't usually pay much attention to the names, but in several cases she'd noticed that they had been indigents, people who'd been sent to Brown by the coroner's office for cremation. Bittner had just assumed it was okay to cut them up. After all, many of them didn't even have families. But now she wasn't so sure.

Bittner could hear Brown trooping in and out of the refrigerator. Allen Tyler was due back in a week. Brown had already piled up corpses in the cooler in preparation for his arrival. There must have been at least fifteen of them, Bittner thought, growing more anxious now. Looking around, she gathered all of the papers from the new cases that had come in and started to go through them, one by one. *I've got two signed Bio-Tech consent forms here*, she remembers thinking. *And last week I may have filed two. So we're looking at four Bio-Tech cases, maybe.* She paused and glanced at the doorway. *Where are the eleven extra bodies coming from?*

chapter 3

The "Toolers"

Word traveled fast about Bio-Tech Anatomical. Allen Tyler made sure everyone knew about the company. If anyone called him at the University of Texas Medical Branch looking for body parts, he simply referred them to Mike Brown. Soon everyone in the market for parts knew about the unusually fertile source of corpses in southern California, and the orders started pouring in.

Most of the buyers were medical-device companies, or "toolers," as Brown called them. "You ever go into a doctor's office and the drug reps are trying to get their product into the doctor? Well, the same thing happens in tooling for surgery," he said. "It's the best way to get the product in front of the doctors. I've got a plane ticket for you, I'm going to put you up at the best hotel and give you cadavers to work on, but you've got to use my product. Nine out of ten of those doctors will leave there and buy those tools."

The buyers included such surgical-equipment companies as Johnson & Johnson, Arthrex, Richard Wolf, Pacific Surgical, Arthrotek, and Nuvasive. They also included brokers, like Perna, who contract to provide a kind of deluxe corpse service to some of the same companies, transporting the parts, setting them up, keeping them fresh, and hauling them away at the end of a seminar.

Tyler had one of the easiest sales jobs around. The customers came to him. For example, on September 29, 2000, he got an e-mail from Neil Crawford, Ph.D., the lab coordinator for Spinal Biomechanics at the Barrow Neurological Institute in Phoenix, Arizona. It said: "Allen, when we talked last, you said you thought a company on the west coast might have specimens that they could sell us. Any word on that? They have not contacted me. We still need several more specimens, especially with the skull base intact, and would be very appreciative."

Tyler replied the same day: "Neil, I am Ccing Michael Brown with Bio-Tech Anatomical. He will be in touch with you on Monday regarding inventory in stock."

Crawford would later buy twenty-two cervical spines from Brown and pay him $13,200. Tyler made $5,000 from the transaction, for the two weekends that it took him to dismember twenty-two bodies.

Every day, the fax machine churned out more orders:

One knee specimen, two shoulder specimens. Please wrap individually.

Per our conversation this afternoon, I am in need of 10 knee, 10 shoulder and 1 wrist specimen.

Two cadaver torsos, preferably female in their sixties, weighing 150 pounds. Must not have had any spinal surgeries.

From her desk, Jennifer Bittner could hear Brown on the phone. "Not a problem," he assured the callers. "We'll get them to you right away." Then, like an eager kid, he bounded up the stairs, packaged the parts in a Styrofoam box, and sent them off.

Bittner still hadn't mentioned her worries to Brown. In fact, she'd tried to forget about the incident with Ronald King. Having grown up around drug addicts, she was used to vague suspicions and, dreading the inevitable disappointment, she'd grown expert at talking herself out of them. In Brown's case, it was easy. *Mike knows what he's doing,* she told herself. *He wouldn't jeopardize his company or get into trouble. He's a businessman. Besides,* she thought, *maybe he got permission.*

The buyers were equally trusting of Brown. They didn't ask questions, and Brown never told them more than they needed to know. This type of arrangement is typical in the underground cadaver trade. Donor names are considered confidential, so buyers never see consent forms. They get a list of ID numbers and a package of parts, and they take the supplier's word for the rest.

If they order through a broker, they may not even know where the parts come from. One of Brown's clients, a company called Arthrotek, which has offices in Ontario, California, ordered shoulders through a San Francisco broker named Michelle Johnson. Johnson, in turn, ordered the shoulders from Brown. An unknown third company delivered the shoulders in a white van to the Arthrotek offices. The driver slipped the package to the Arthrotek employee and both men went on their way.

By the summer of 2000, just six months after founding Bio-Tech, Brown was making plans to open another willed-body company. Brown was a proponent of "diversifying." As he put it, "Multiple things means multiple money." But he had another good reason to diversify. He needed someplace to hide the earnings from Bio-Tech. Each week, Brown received checks for thousands of dollars. But Bio-Tech got just one donated body a week.

A new company would provide a new bank account, new bills, everything he'd need to explain away the money he was making from stolen bodies. Now he just needed a partner. An excellent prospect was his son's roller hockey coach, John Schultz. Schultz was a placid man who made a living repairing laser tools. Brown saw him as a "typical middle-class guy, picket fence, green grass, one boy and one girl."

Like other people who are tempted by the cadaver trade, Schultz was looking for an easy way to earn some extra cash. He made a good living, but he was worried he wouldn't have enough to put his kids through college. He hadn't taken them on a vacation trip in years. He thought maybe he'd start a little business on the side.

In the summer of 2000, John Schultz almost bought a gas station. *Everyone needs gas,* he told himself. *You don't need to be a marketing genius to sell the product—just make sure you have a big sign on a good corner.* Schultz could hire someone to run the station for him, pay all his bills, and still clear a nice profit.

But most of the gas stations Schultz looked at cost at least $125,000 up front. That would mean a second mortgage on his house, and he'd probably have to raid his retirement account, too.

One hot, dry day outside Michael Brown's crematorium, Schultz and Brown's conversation about the roller hockey team veered off course. Schultz confessed that he couldn't afford to buy the gas station that he'd looked at that morning.

Michael Brown said suddenly, "Why don't you go into business with me?"

Schultz was startled. *What business?* he wondered. *The crematorium or the funeral home?*

"What do you mean?" he asked, trying to be cautious around this very successful man.

But already he knew that he badly wanted to accept. Michael Brown was making real money—and having fun at it.

"We'll start an anatomical business," Brown said.

"But I don't know anything about that," Schultz replied.

Brown patted his new buddy on the back. "Don't worry about it," he said. "I'll pay for everything."

In September 2000, with Brown's help, Schultz incorporated California Bio-Science. Brown found a storefront office for the new company in Temecula, twenty minutes away, and suggested that Schultz write up a newspaper ad. "Here's what you've got to say," he explained. "You could spend thousands of dollars for a funeral, hundreds of dollars on a cremation, or you could donate your body for free."

Even with the ad, California Bio-Science got just six legitimate bodies in five months. During the same time, Brown deposited $156,638.14 from his dubious business into the account.

Things were going well for Bio-Tech. Brown was becoming the sort of man he always knew himself to be. He bought himself a new Ford F350 truck. He tinted the windows and had the chassis lifted so that he could drive high up off the ground. The modest house where he lived with his family in a quiet cul-de-sac wasn't right for the new life he had fashioned. So he rented it out and bought a plot of land near a horse farm. He planned to build a ranch for himself and his wife and their boys. In the meantime, they lived in a tract home on their new property.

The better things went, the more reckless Brown became. By midfall, no body was safe. As soon as Daniel Schonberger unloaded a new delivery of corpses to be cremated from the van, Brown told Terrazas and Schultz to go through their papers. He said, "Pull all the ones under fifty-five."

If there weren't enough, Brown became angry.

"Forget fifty-five and under," he yelled. "Take anybody."

With these instructions, Terrazas hauled any corpse entrusted to Brown's crematorium into the embalming room and Tyler dismembered it. Many arrived from funeral homes that had hired Brown to perform their cremations. Among these bodies was the corpse of AIDs victim, Jim Farrelly. Though skeletal and diseased, he, too, was chosen for the cutting table as were countless others who were supposed to be cremated and returned to their families.

Terrazas burned what remained of the bodies in a box in the oven. When it was time to send urns to the families, Brown said, "Go make up some ashes." Terrazas divvied up the ashes from the oven, bagged them, and didn't ask questions.

Toward the end of the summer, Jennifer Bittner had gone on maternity leave. Her gynecologist had ordered bed rest. Brown gave her money for maternity clothes, paid her disability, and advanced her cash. A new office manager had taken her place, a divorcée named Kathie Ross, who either didn't notice what was going on or just never bothered to say anything.

Other people came and went during 2000, including the state crematorium inspector, Dan Redmond. Redmond didn't notice anything unusual. The crematorium was still spotless. The files appeared to be in order. Redmond knew about Bio-Tech, but he didn't see it as a problem. When Brown mentioned that he planned to offer free cremations

in poor Hispanic neighborhoods in exchange for body donations, it seemed like further evidence of his caring nature.
While most guys were inflating their prices, Mike Brown
was helping out his families.

Brown might have gone on indefinitely had it not been
for the suspicions of a neighboring businessman, Doug
Lada. Lada owned a storefront funeral home in the nearby
town of Rancho Cucamonga. He didn't have a lot of space
besides an office, so Brown let him use his embalming room to
prepare bodies. In exchange, Lada lent Brown an embalming machine and gave him all of his cremation business.

In early December 2000, Lada dropped in at the crematorium to prepare a body for an upcoming funeral. As
usual, Brown's embalming room was shiny and clean. Lada
laid the cardboard box carrying the corpse on one of the
gurneys. He removed the wax paper covering the top of the
body and dropped it into a red plastic bag used for biohaz-
ard waste. Since the bag was full, Lada tied it up.

"Hey, Louie, what should I do with this thing?" he
called out, holding up the bag.

Terrazas pointed to a cardboard box beside the oven.
"Just put it in there," he said, and went back to work.

At first, Lada wasn't sure what he was looking at. There
was a body inside the box, but something was odd about it.
He lifted the lid a little farther and saw that it contained the
body of a man. But the body was missing its shoulders, and
a pair of arms rested between its legs.

Lada glanced at Louie, who was in the process of incinerating a body, and closed the box. He noted the name of the funeral home written on the side as Caring Cremation. There was only one reason that a funeral home like Caring Cremation sent a body to Brown, and that was to have it cremated. Lada wondered why this man had been dismembered. But he didn't say anything. He simply wrote a note to himself and left.

Brown, meanwhile, was getting ready for the annual holiday party for funeral directors. He'd already reserved a table at a country club in San Diego. All of his funeral-home clients would be there, including the people from Caring Cremation. Brown left his wife at home with the kids and joined his employees.

He arrived at the club feeling smug, dressed in a turtleneck and an olive-green suit. If anyone belonged at a country club, surely it was he. Brown had just bought a new boat and a BMW. That evening, he worked the room, Scotch in hand, boasting and bluffing his way though the crowd of current and potential clients.

Jennifer Bittner tagged along beside him. After giving birth to a baby boy, she was svelte again. Brown gazed at her shapely body. After the party, Kathie Ross invited Brown and the others back to her house for more merriment. There, Brown and Bittner had sex.

Christmas passed without incident. Brown helped his son decorate their new house with $600 worth of lights. New Year's came and went.

On the evening of January 8, 2001, Doug Lada stopped

by Brown's crematorium again. This time, he had come to pick up some ashes. The lights were on inside when Lada pulled up in the parking lot. When he opened the door, he saw an open cardboard coffin lying on the cement floor. The bottom was stained and the cardboard was torn, as if the body inside had been too heavy to lift and someone had dragged it out onto the floor. Lada looked around but saw no one. Then he headed for the embalming room.

He wasn't prepared for what he found. There, on the metal gurneys, were two bloody, dismembered bodies, one belonging to a young woman. Her head, which still had all of her brown hair, had been cut from its socket, and it lay beside her torso. A toe tag lay on the table, and Lada noticed that the name on it matched the name written on the outside of the box in the other room.

"Hey, Doug. How you doing?"

Lada turned. There was Brown standing by the door, dressed in pale blue scrubs and smiling. His shoes were splattered with blood.

"Fine, fine," Lada replied. He grabbed the urn of ashes that he had come for and left. Again, he wrote a note to himself.

Several weeks passed. Jennifer Bittner was now back at work, helping Kathie Ross with the growing amount of paperwork, but she'd started to feel guilty. Things were supposed to be different now that she had a son, and she wished she hadn't cheated. It bothered her so much, in fact, that she confessed the drunken affair with Brown to Steve McCarty, her son's father.

He was not sympathetic.

"What kind of shit are you pulling?" he yelled. "I don't have time for playing games like this." Within minutes, he was on the phone to Brown. The two men argued. Later, McCarty told Bittner that if she didn't quit her job, he would leave her and take their son.

He said, "You committed adultery, and they'll give that kid to me."

Terrified, Bittner turned in her final time sheet and didn't return to work. Hoping to find a new job, she called Doug Lada.

"Hey, Doug," she said. "Do you know anyone who's hiring?"

Lada said he did not. He paused for a moment and started to say something about his suspicions concerning Brown, but Bittner interrupted him.

"You don't need to go any further," she said. "I already know what you're talking about."

Lada would later tell Bittner that if she ever decided to go forward about Brown, he'd back her 100 percent. Bittner thought about it and then, a week after she quit, Brown sent her a threatening letter. Not only did he refuse to release her final paycheck, but he demanded she pay back the $1,350 he had advanced her during her pregnancy.

"Simple math," he wrote. "You owe this company."

Bittner was twenty years old, unmarried, with little money and a new baby. She was confused and desperate. When she confided in her friends about Brown, they told her to blackmail him, but she was reluctant. She knew

Brown well, and she suspected he had been careful to cover his tracks.

One day, on her way home from her new job at a funeral home, Bittner found herself driving in the direction of the Riverside County Coroner's Office, where her friend Carol Gallagher worked transcribing medical records. As she drove, she debated whether to tell her friend everything.

As soon as she sat down, she turned to Gallagher and said, "Are you in a sworn position where if I tell you something you have to tell one of the deputy sheriffs here?"

Gallagher looked worried.

"It's not murder. It's not anything like that."

———

Detective Rene Rodriguez took notes on a pad while his boss briefed him. Rodriguez is a short, compact Texan. He has shiny black hair, a mustache, and the stolid expression of a TV detective. Around headquarters, he's known for his persistence on tough cases and his obsession with the Old West. The other detectives used to tease him about his office, where framed paintings of cowboys, Indians, and horses lined the walls. Hanging near Rodriguez's desk was a poster of the country singer Terri Clark.

In his twenty-year career, Detective Rodriguez had worked every kind of case—pimps, homicides, crooked cops, serial killers; he'd seen them all. So far, this case was unlike anything he'd ever heard of. Rodriguez leaned back in his chair and twirled his pen. "Go on," he said to Sergeant Mullins.

"The informant is a young woman, a former employee. Possibly disgruntled," Mullins said, reading from the manila folder on his lap. "She says this guy is cutting up body parts in the back of his crematorium." Mullins added that Brown had a contract with the county coroner to cremate the bodies of indigents. This was something they needed to move on fast.

Rodriguez dialed his partner, Dave Fernandez. Then he called Dan Redmond, the state crematorium inspector. Redmond had already been briefed about the story by someone at the coroner's office. He wasn't buying it. Mike Brown? Selling body parts? Not a chance in hell. Rodriguez didn't tell Redmond much, just that they needed to meet and talk to this woman, a former employee at a crematorium.

The next night, Redmond met Rodriguez and Fernandez, and followed Rodriguez's unmarked, dark green Chevy Impala through a rainstorm to the small town of Temecula, where Bittner lived with her aunt and her baby in a small apartment.

After twenty years on the job, Rodriguez could suss out a person in minutes—by the cadence of their voice, if they blanched or blushed, and so on. Bittner, he noticed, was matter-of-fact, even calm, when she came to the door. She invited them into her tidy living room, and she looked right at Rodriguez. Rodriguez thought: *Let's see what she's got.* He turned on his tape recorder.

"This is Investigator Rene Rodriguez," he announced into the machine. "I'm with the Riverside Sheriff's Department.

62   BODY BROKERS

Today's date is the twenty-seventh of February, the year
2001. . . . We're currently at Jennifer Bittner's residence. . . .
We're in the process of interviewing her to obtain additional
information concerning an individual by the name of Michael
Brown."

Bittner told them everything.

Inspector Redmond sat on the couch, staring in disbelief.
Bittner described how Tyler had dismembered the bodies.
She told them about her affair with Brown. Redmond wondered how this could have happened. Mike Brown wasn't
the kind of guy to do anything like this. But the more Bittner talked, the more detail she provided, the more Redmond thought maybe he'd been wrong about Brown.

"Why do you think he was doing this?" he asked her.

"He got greedy," Bittner replied matter-of-factly. "He
saw the money that could be made. I mean, when you guys
find the invoices, you'll see why."

"If you knew all this was occurring . . . why hadn't you
reported [it] . . . earlier?" Rodriguez asked her.

"I was scared to ruin people's lives," she said.

Bittner said there was a "witness" who could corrobo-
rate her story, and she gave Rodriguez the phone number
and address of Doug Lada. After two hours with Lada,
Rodriguez was ready to apply for a search warrant. Two
days later, a caravan of police cars and refrigerated trucks
descended on the crematorium.

Brown was out at his ranch digging a new well when
Rodriguez burst through the door of the crematorium. Within
minutes, Rodriguez and his partners were upstairs in the attic.

What they found resembled a butcher shop. A corpse, destined for Augie Perna, lay on the wood floor in a puddle of blood. Lined up along the wall were seven meat freezers. One of the freezers contained shoulders. Another held elbows, another torsos, another spines, and yet another knees, among which were the knees of Jim Farrelly. Each cut of flesh had been wrapped and labeled. The detectives were startled when they lifted the door of one freezer and found sets of eyes staring back at them through plastic wrap. The heads still had all of their hair and teeth.

Stuffed inside two of the freezers were two whole bodies, their legs bent slightly at the knees. When detectives laid the bodies on the plywood floor, they rocked back and forth like wooden horses.

———

In October 2003, Michael Brown, who pocketed more than four hundred thousand dollars from sales of body parts, pleaded guilty to sixty-six counts of mutilation of human remains and embezzlement. On October 3, the families of his victims gathered in a sandstone courthouse in Murrieta, California, a dusty desert town sixty-five miles northeast of San Diego.

Almost a year had passed since Jim Farrelly's mother, Joyce, received the phone call from the victim's advocate. It had taken months for the news to set in. Then, the nightmares started. In one recurring dream, Jim's head appeared and spoke to her. "Please make this stop," he pleaded.

Since then, Joyce had learned that the funeral home,

where Jim had made his arrangements, used Michael Brown to do their cremations. In her grief, Joyce hadn't read the cremation forms closely. But even if she had, Pacific Crematorium would have meant nothing to her. "It could have said Joe Blow Fireworks," she said, "The question never came into my mind as to how the details worked. Jim had given his wishes, and I thought that the funeral home would see to it that it was done."

In the courtroom, one by one, the families rose. Brown sat just a few feet away, but he didn't turn to look at Joyce when she got up to speak.

"After all Jim did to protect us from any further grief, Mr. Brown, you took it all away," Joyce cried. "You destroyed that for us."

Brown stared ahead, his eyes fixed coldly on the judge.

"Jim had AIDS. Was he concerned about that when he butchered . . . his body parts?" Joyce asked the judge. "Does he even care?"

Jim's sister, Joy, had also prepared a speech. But she was too distraught to speak. Others rose to take their places.

"Even with the horrible pain of losing my mom," one woman said, "I was comforted knowing I kept my promises to her. You took my promise of dignity and grace, and in the final moments you made me a liar."

It wasn't simply that loved ones had been brutally dismembered, or that the families hadn't given Brown permission to use the bodies. It was more than that. Michael Brown had violated their memory, and there was no way to get that back.

"The last time I saw my mother, she was in the viewing room," said one woman named Ruth Storr. "She looked so peaceful, like she was asleep. She had no pain on her face. Her skin was soft as a baby's bottom. . . . I told her I loved her and thanked her for being my mother."

No matter that her mother's spirit had long since departed. Lois Storr's corpse retained its beloved features; the limber typist's hands with which she held her daughter, the slender arms that she used to comfort and hug her, the lips with which she kissed her. In Ruth's imagination, her mother's body was inseparable from her memory.

She said of Brown in disbelief: "He carved her up like a side of beef."

Judge Rodney Walker sentenced Brown to twenty years in prison.

———

Shortly after Brown's sentencing, I wrote to him requesting an interview. Brown responded immediately and, against the advice of his lawyers, invited me to come to California so that we could meet, as he put it, *"facie ad faciem."*

It was dark on the day that I visited Brown. A heavy fog hovered over the low concrete buildings of North Kern State Prison in Delano, a farm town two hours north of Los Angeles. From a distance, the soaring streetlamps placed at intervals around the barren landscape made the prison look almost cheerful, like an amusement park, its bright lights blaring through the mist on the outskirts of town.

At the entrance to the prison, I waited with a group of hungry-looking women for the warden to open the doors. When we finally got inside, a short, beefy guard sent me through to a visiting area where inmates sat holding hands with their girlfriends, and ushered me to a chair in the back beside a telephone. Unlike the other prisoners at North Kern, Brown was being held in what's known as "reception," a kind of quarantine, before being placed in a permanent prison. He wasn't allowed to have physical contact with any visitors, and I had to speak to him by phone through a glass partition.

After about ten minutes, the door to the cubicle behind the partition opened and a tall, muscular man in an orange jumpsuit appeared. Michael Brown has short, sandy blond hair shaved in a buzz cut, a narrow face, and a prominent nose. He stared straight at me through the glass, locking his blue eyes into mine, and reached for the receiver on the phone. There was a lean aggression about him that instantly set me on edge. He pressed his face close to the glass, so close that I could see the colony of tiny capillaries where the blood had burst through on the tip of his nose.

Over the next three days, Brown and I talked for a total of eight hours. Tape recorders are prohibited at North Kern, so I had to take notes as he spoke, balancing the telephone receiver between my ear and my shoulder. This made observing him difficult. When I looked up, I was met by his probing stare. Brown spoke in a monotone. Most of the time, he addressed me as "Ms. Cheney." Occasionally, though, when he wanted to plead his goodness, he called me by my first name.

"I need to let you know where my heart's at, and the true conviction that I had to serve," he said. "It was an incredible injustice, and it never should have happened. If a body is not donated, you don't chop it up and sell off the body parts. I can't make it any clearer than that, Annie."

So what happened? I asked.

"I was the captain of that ship," he said. "But I let other people captain it."

"What do you mean by that?"

"I had a lot of unethical people around me, and I should've been smarter. I should've fired them on the spot for the wrongful disarticulation of human remains," he said, rubbing his nose.

"But you pled guilty."

Brown smiled. "You obviously don't understand the concept of pleading guilty. Jennifer Bittner doesn't tell a lot of truth," he added. "She's a Jerry Springer candidate."

Brown spent several hours trying to explain the crime that had landed him in prison. Mostly, he blamed others. "Once our company incorporated and once we received the donations, it was evident that we were not going to have enough material," he said. "We were receiving one hundred orders a day, and we were only able to fill two. Instead of telling the customer no, I would refer them to Augie or Allen. Allen Tyler made sure that I had plenty of material."

He paused for a moment, eyeing my expression. "Now,

don't get me wrong, Annie," he went on, "my eyes were open all the time. . . . I don't want to sound like the victim. I knew that when that first package came from UTMB [University of Texas Medical Branch], we were headed in the wrong direction. Anyone scrambling around on training wheels looking for a mentor would have known that."

"So you're saying Allen Tyler sent you body parts?" I asked.

"He sent me hundreds and hundreds and hundreds of body parts," Brown replied.

"So who made the money?" I asked.

"We did."

According to the Riverside district attorney, there is no evidence that Allen Tyler or Augie Perna sent body parts to Brown's business for any reason other than to be cremated after a conference. But Brown was adamant. "They were my partners. They were officers in my companies," he said, his voice rising. "Those two were distanced from me as if I was the mastermind to take some Frankenstein lab and to swindle people out of their loved ones' remains. I can tell you that Allen Tyler and Augie Perna did a masterful job of alienating themselves in case of the fall. And we all know that the fall did come."

At other times, Brown seemed to blame the business itself. "The brutality involved in the anatomical world deadens your nerves," he said at one point. "My son said, 'Dad, I can't get through this in my heart. Cutting up dead people?'" Brown shook his head. "Some people never get through that. Once you cross over to the unethical area, then I don't think you look at dignity anymore."

This sort of indifference held true for the brokers who tempted him and the buyers who played along, he said. "They could've cared less. They needed the material and they sent me the check. I had plane tickets given to me. Clothing. Cases of wine!" he said. "The money you could make was incredible. It was like putting a mountain of money in a field and no one accounting for it."

Even if he was guilty, what difference did it make? "One way or another someone makes money off of the dead," Brown pointed out. "Funeral homes, they're all for profit." Besides, whether you cut up the bodies or not, death is an unpleasant business. "When you drive by a funeral home and you see those signs that say that stuff about dignity and care? There's no dignity in death," he said, wagging his finger at me. "The body purges, it bloats, and it bleeds. The embalming process is a mutilation of the body. I've seen it! There is not one mortuary in southern California that I would choose to go to when I pass away. Put me in a boat. Light it with fuel and send me off like the Vikings."

———

On Saturday, I visited Brown's old crematorium. One of his former clients had taken over the business after Brown was arrested, and I had heard that he had hired Louie Terrazas to stay on and do the cremations. This seemed like a peculiar decision, since Terrazas had been charged with one count of conspiracy and was sentenced to a year in the county jail, which he served by working at a road camp. But sure enough, when I called the crematorium, Terrazas answered the phone. I told him that I was interested in getting a tour, and he agreed to meet me.

The sun was setting as I pulled off Interstate 15 and made a right onto a dead-end street and into the empty parking lot, where Terrazas was waiting for me. It was quiet except for the caw of a distant bird. On this brisk February evening, Terrazas was dressed in army shorts, a white, short-sleeved, button-down shirt, and sandals.

"Everything's the same. Nothing's changed," he said, referring to the decor as he unlocked the door and reached inside for the light switch, illuminating a large, white-tiled foyer. The cavernous room was empty except for a small Formica box in the center, which someone had decorated with a plastic fern.

"We used to have a brass dolphin fountain in the middle there," Terrazas said, pointing to the table. In the corner, he showed me where Brown kept his fish tank. Then he led me into a kitchen, where he helped himself to a can of Bud Light.

"You want something?" he asked.

"No, thanks," I said.

To the right of the foyer was a chapel. A reproduction of *The Last Supper* hung on the wall. Terrazas led me along a long, narrow hallway to the crematorium, a large garage-like room with two retractable metal doors. To the right of the doors were three cremation ovens, vaguely resembling commercial pizza ovens, with cylindrical stacks leading up and out through the roof.

On the west side of the room was a narrow white door leading to the embalming room. Affixed to the door was a plaque with the following message:

REMEMBER: Behind these doors is the most sacred room in the building. It is where loved ones come to be prepared for the most difficult event in a family's life. Those that work behind these doors pledge to each family a never-ending commitment of respect and service to those that place their trust in us.

Terrazas giggled as he looked up at the plaque. Then, glancing at me, he shook his head and said, "I read that thing every day and I think, What a bunch of bullshit."

Inside the embalming room were two metal gurneys and, behind them, two porcelain sinks. On the opposite wall was a cabinet containing boxes of paper surgical gowns and shoe covers.

Next to the embalming room was the walk-in refrigerator. A piece of paper was taped to the door. In typewritten letters it read: "Every job is a self-portrait of the person who does it. Autograph your work with excellence."

Below it was another sign: "Daniel was preferred above the presidents and princes because an excellent spirit was in him."

"Why was *Daniel* preferred?" I asked Louie.

"Because an excellent spirit was in him."

"That's not a reference to Brown's employee Daniel Schonberger?" I asked.

"No," Terrazas said. "It's just a verse from the Bible."

He opened the door to the refrigerator. The room was damp and stale.

"I'm afraid I'm going to see a ghost," I said.

"Your mind plays with you," he said.

Metal racks lined the right-hand wall of the refrigerator, where there were a few long cardboard boxes containing bodies, I presumed. We stood there for a moment, and then Terrazas showed me the machine for morselizing bone left over after a cremation. The machine, which is common to crematoria, was a small metal bowl with an electrical blade on the bottom, not unlike a food processor's. Terrazas explained that after the ashes cool, he whirrs them up in the morselizer until he's achieved a powdery dust. Families are more comfortable receiving fine dust than dust with hunks of bone. But this very same process makes identifying the remains difficult. The process of cremation destroys all DNA, and without bone fragments, it is hard to tell if the ashes are even those of a human. "Don't you want to see the upstairs?" Terrazas said suddenly, as if I had forgotten the best part.

"Sure."

"Okay. I'm going to have to get another beer for that." Terrazas retrieved another Bud Light from the refrigerator, and I followed him up the stairs.

At the top, lined up in a row along the wall, were the meat freezers. Terrazas nodded at them as if to say, "I told you this was no joke." Taped to the top of each freezer was a small, square piece of paper on which was a number written in black marker. Terrazas opened #5.

The inside was deep red, like dried blood, though it was only rust.

"When my new boss took over, we dumped all kinds of bleach in them to get rid of the stench," Terrazas explained.

"What did they smell like?" I asked.

"Like something gone bad—real bad."

When I opened #4, the odor made me gag. It was sour, like spoiled meat.

Styrofoam coolers were piled in the corner.

"Are those left over from when Brown owned the place?" I asked him.

"Yeah," Terrazas said.

On our way back to his office, Terrazas stopped suddenly at the door to the embalming room. He looked around nervously.

"Right now I remember the noise that the saw made. A hand saw," he said "Like when I would go and get a body in the cooler, I would hear that noise, you know? I never heard that noise before."

"Does it bother you to think of it now?" I asked him.

"I don't think about it," he said. Terrazas got another beer—his third in less than two hours—and I left.

On Sunday, Brown was jumpy when he arrived for our interview. He kept rubbing his chin and blinking. "I stayed awake last night and I thought, Why did I do this?" he said. "The accentuation of the tragedy is the fact that we were so honorable."

Like many criminals, Brown blames his victims. Corpses are vulnerable, he tried to tell me. They're just asking for it. Anyone would be tempted. "Right before Nixon resigned, he looked at the portrait of Kennedy and he said, 'People will look at you and wonder who they can be and they will look at me and know what they really are.'"

"What do you mean by that?" I asked him.

"People look at me as Frankenstein and a ghoul and they know what they are," he said, glaring at me. "Kennedy was just as much a crook as Nixon. Both fell from grace. Every man and woman goes to the altar and says, 'Do I want to go right or left?' And the greater responsibility you have, the greater the chance it is that you'll slip up."

Brown said the cadaver trade is rife with people who "slip up." He said it was the nature of the game, since demand for body parts is high, supply is low, and dead bodies don't talk. "We all have a line in the sand, Annie," he said, "and people in the anatomical business have an eraser in their right hand and a stick in their left, and that line is moved daily. Daily!"

I asked if it was possible to regulate the business. He thought for a few moments and then shook his head.

"There won't be any regulation. The only regulations that stay true are the ones that someone had an aggressive conviction about, like the mother that loses her child to a drunk driver."

In the visiting room, someone had switched on a boom box. In the glass, I could see the reflection of an inmate dancing to some obscure fifties tune.

Brown leaned in to the window. He said, "It would be an arduous task to try and regulate it. You're going to have lobbyists like J and J. It's not going to happen. These toolers don't want regulation."

"Could you ever remove the profit from it?" I asked.

"Not in a capitalistic society. There are a lot of little naturalists banging their little boats into oil tankers. It's not my idea of how to do things, but they'll try. In the end," Brown said, "they're not going to succeed. There's too much money to be made."

chapter 4

"As Soon as You Die, You're Mine"

In Miami, Augie Perna stood in the conference room of the Trump International Sonesta Beach Resort. Looking out the picture window, Perna studied the swimming pool, where children were playing and women were tanning, and gazed at the pale blue ocean beyond. Then he closed the drapes. In the dimness, he and two other men took six large ice-filled coolers from the corner and unpacked them. From each one they lifted a plastic-wrapped torso. They laid them on gurneys. Then, like an expert tailor arranging fabric for a suit, Perna turned back the plastic and taped the torsos in place.

A broker is only as good as his source. Luckily for Perna, after Michael Brown was arrested, he had no trouble finding a new supplier. Perna now gets most of his torsos from an Arizona company called ScienceCare Anatomical, which supplied all of the torsos for the seminar I attended in Miami.

ScienceCare was founded by a man named James E. Rogers four months after Brown started Bio-Tech Anatomical. Brown said he met "Jimmy" while Rogers was working as a salesman for Mission Life Insurance. According to Brown, Rogers stopped by his crematorium looking for new clients. The two men started talking business, he said, and soon Brown was bragging about his success with Bio-Tech. Rogers, according to Brown, was intrigued. "I've never seen anyone so excited as he was," Brown said. "Jimmy was like a rocket off of a launching pad. He took it and went with it. I don't know whether it was the money or his own entrepreneurial spirit that got him to do it," Brown said. "But you know, the entrepreneurial spirit can't be tamed."

Rogers denies ever meeting or knowing Brown. But during their search of Brown's crematorium, Riverside detectives seized a letter from Rogers to Brown in which Rogers thanked Brown for taking the time to meet with him. In the letter, Rogers enumerated the laws in place regarding anatomical donations and their penalties, specifically pointing out the prohibition on buying and selling body parts. "This is another good reason to charge procurement and processing fees etc. as opposed to fees for a specific tissue," he wrote to Brown. In a postscript, Rogers asked, "What do you think of the logo, my friend?" ScienceCare's logo at that point consisted of three miniature symbols: the Washington Monument, an atom, and a copy of an anatomical drawing by Leonardo Da Vinci.

ScienceCare opened in June 2000. Thanks to an aggressive marketing campaign, within two years the company was selling body parts to major surgical-equipment companies such as Arthrex and Smith & Nephew—big companies with a great need for corpses.

ScienceCare has modernized the corpse-recruiting process. Unlike Brown's company, whose corpses presented themselves, ScienceCare obtains donations by advertising in the newspaper and at senior citizen conventions and sending its employees to nursing homes and hospice centers in and around Arizona to pitch the perks of donation. These include free transportation for every corpse, free filing of death certificates, and a free cremation, a value of approximately $500. The company advertises in the yellow pages under Cremation: ScienceCare Anatomical Inc. "Cremation at No Cost."

Unlike medical schools, which reject autopsied or obese bodies or the bodies of people who have died of certain diseases, ScienceCare is somewhat flexible. Though the company rejects bodies infected with HIV and hepatitis, it has no limits on age or size, and if a body is missing an organ or some other part, the company can always find a home for the rest. The company has advertised this fact freely, sending letters and faxes to medical schools and offering to take bodies that they refuse, though most medical schools have been reluctant to refer families to a for-profit company.

ScienceCare's success has spawned a branch in Denver and a similar company in Oregon called BioGift, which is owned by a former ScienceCare employee.

———

Perna stood for a moment in the Ocean Room, his petite hands on his hips, admiring the torso at Station 1, which was so tiny it could have been mistaken for that of a child. The arms and legs had been removed, and the stumps that remained exposed curly masses of veins and muscles. "See here?" he said, gesturing matter-of-factly with his hands. "This is where the arms would be. And the legs—they would be there. But we don't need the legs for this type of thing. That would be wasteful."

Like other brokers, Perna rarely buys a whole corpse. It's cheaper for him to just get the parts that he needs, and it's more profitable for companies like ScienceCare, which can sell the legs and arms and heads to someone else. Corpses are precious commodities, and once dismembered, each one goes much farther than it would have had it been left intact.

Perna buys his torsos precut and frozen from Science-Care and has them shipped from Arizona to his warehouse in Allentown, Pennsylvania. He keeps fifty or sixty torsos on hand, each of which takes about four days to defrost. The thaw time varies with the size of the corpse, which means it varies a good deal. "Look at that one over there," Perna said, pointing to a beach ball of a torso in the corner. "Look at how much larger that one is."

———

Augie Perna got his start in the body-parts business through pigs. In the mid-1990s, a veterinarian friend gave him a job at his company, Worldwide Mobile Vet. The company, Perna said, bought live pigs from farms in southern California and elsewhere and trucked them to medical-training seminars at hotels, universities, and hospitals around the country. For decades, live pigs were the specimen of choice for educating surgeons. Their anatomy is amazingly close to that of a human being and like a human patient under anesthesia, but unlike a corpse, pigs bleed. During the 1990s, as courses in surgery began to focus on minimally invasive techniques, anatomical correctness became more important than the propensity to bleed.

Perna saw an opportunity. "This was something that I thought would always be around, because all of the new procedures that are coming out on the market are minimally invasive." Cadavers were both more profitable—$1,500 for a torso versus $250 for a pig—and, being inanimate, easier to handle. "Businesswise," Perna said, "the returns are there."

In 1995, Perna founded his first company, Limbs & Things—the name was later changed to the more tasteful Surgical Body Forms. Three years later, he started IMET and, a year after that, a sister company, Mobile Medical Training Unit. IMET hosts half a dozen educational courses per year.

But the bulk of Perna's income comes from supplying surgical-equipment companies and doctors with body parts to use in seminars. Perna offers them a top-drawer corpse service, transporting the parts, setting them up, keeping them fresh, and hauling them away. The companies reward him handsomely. "I'm doing a course for cancer where they want the bodies from the head all the way down to the midtibia," he said. "That ticket? Sixty-eight thousand dollars! I make, like, $15,000 after it's all said and done—for one day's worth of work."

Providing this type of service requires a certain amount of skill, particularly in the area of corpse maintenance. "Once we defrost the [torsos], the liquid comes out," Perna said. "We also give them what you call a bowel prep."

I asked him how one goes about prepping a bowel.

"With a device that we designed. We go up the rectum."

Here I must have flinched, because Perna touched my arm softly, as if to soothe me. "You see, the moment you die, you have a bowel movement," he said. "We take care of that."

It's not every man who would give a corpse an enema. Consequently, competition in Perna's field is scarce. But the opportunities are substantial. There are hundreds of educational seminars held every year by associations, hospitals, universities, and educational companies like IMET. While many of these consist simply of lectures and slides, others, targeted at surgeons, offer "hands-on training" with body parts.

No one keeps track of exactly how many courses feature anatomical specimens, but Florida, a popular state for training seminars, provides some clues. Florida is the only state in the country that requires vendors to get approval from the state anatomy board before shipping in parts.

Florida state records show that in 2003, there were twenty-one requests to the board by companies and doctors who wanted to import body parts for surgical-training seminars. All twenty-one requests were approved, and over the course of the year, seventy-six heads and necks, eighty-three shoulders, thirty-four whole cadavers, thirty-two torsos, eighteen legs, ten knees, eight hands, six forearms, and one cervical spine crossed the border into Florida. In 1995, there were just two requests.

Every year, dozens of body parts enter the state undetected. Indeed, according to Dr. Lynn Romrell, the director of the Anatomical Board of Florida, Augie Perna never sought approval to bring his torsos to the Trump.

Companies that market minimally invasive technology—like Zimmer, Medtronic Sofamor Danek, Ethicon Endosurgery, Stryker Endoscopy, and US Surgical, to name just a few—not only hold conferences in hotels, hospitals, and universities, but some have also built their own institutes, where surgeons can attend courses showcasing the company's devices.

In 2003, for example, Zimmer spent about $2 million to build a 15,000-square-foot training center in Warsaw, Indiana, for courses in minimally invasive joint replacement; the company plans to create satellite institutes around the world. Ethicon Endosurgery, a division of Johnson & Johnson, already has three institutes—in Hamburg, Tokyo, and Cincinnati. For those surgeons who don't want to travel, Medtronic has even transformed a tractor-trailer into a mobile learning center. Surgeons call it "the cadaver truck."

The more hands-on courses that are available, the more the demand for brokers. As Perna explained it, many companies with their own centers won't get involved in the dirty work of corpses. Instead they contract it out to people like him. In some cases, Perna is hired directly by the doctors teaching the seminars.

Records show that he has provided torsos and torso expertise to some of the country's most prominent surgeons. "These doctors are personal friends of mine," he said.

"How did you work that angle?" I asked.

"They're guys," he said. "It's that comradity that we have. You know, I'm not an egghead."

Besides locating reliable suppliers like Brown, Perna also oversees the interstate trafficking of parts. If a customer in Kansas needs a shoulder, Perna will arrange delivery. I asked him how he got the torsos from Pennsylvania to Florida. These he may drive down, he said, but as often as not, he'll simply pack them up like so many Kobe steaks and mail them. He said, "Why reinvent the wheel? You call a freight company and they deal with it."

Perna and ScienceCare have accounts with Airways Freight Corporation, a pioneering middleman in the cadaver trade. Michael Brown was also an Airways client. "We do consider ourselves to be a leader in the movement of anatomical specimens," said the marketing director at Airways, Mike Nimmo. He also said that Airways brokers about eighty body-parts shipments a month, using commercial airlines, FedEx, and UPS. But he was hesitant to provide details. "I don't think the public realizes that these products are being shipped through the general system."

Some shipping professionals are themselves surprised

to find body parts in the mail. In November 2003, FedEx employees in Maplewood, Missouri, noticed that an unmarked package was leaking blood. When they opened the package and two others bound for the same destination, they found a leg and two arms. FedEx prohibits shipping human remains, but their clients do it anyway. In the Missouri case, the shipper was unrepentant. As he told a local reporter, "Boxes break."

In the Ocean Room, one of the doctors himself was struggling with a leaking corpse. "Excuse me a moment," Perna said, and hurried over to help. As I stood watching, a big-bellied guy with a suntan and round metal-rim glasses came over and introduced himself as Mike Charloff, IMET's "Florida person." Charloff was jolly and extraordinarily friendly. "I help them out when they're lacking people," he explained in a smoker's rumble.

We were joined by Dave Myers, a cherubic blonde with a goatee, wearing surgical scrubs like Perna's. "Having fun today?" he asked with apparent sincerity.

"Dave drove down and then stayed at my house for one night," Charloff said. They left the torsos in the car. "I have neighbors across the street that are from Ghana, and if she knew about it she would pack up and leave. She would be like, 'I got to go. I got to go.'" Charloff waved his hands in an approximation of Ghanaian panic.

The quality of the product is important in any business, but it is crucial in the body business, since corpses are in a state of decay. Myers, Charloff, and Perna have developed tricks for preserving the flesh. For example, before freezing a corpse, they massage Vicks VapoRub into the skin. That way when the body defrosts, the odor is of menthol, not old cheese. The most important thing is to keep the body cool. On long drives, they stop regularly at 7-Eleven for ice.

———

On the second morning of the Miami conference, I found Perna alone with his torsos in the Ocean Room. He was spritzing them with bright blue deodorizer from a spray bottle. Overnight, they had acquired a renewed vigor and their skin glistened as a live person's might after a short jog.

"Can I touch one?" I asked him.

"Sure," he said, guiding me to a torso in the corner. Through my plastic glove, the freckled skin of the torso felt cool. The flesh yielded to my fingers like clay.

Perna watched me closely.

"Does this ever get you down?" I asked him.

"The cadavers?"

"Yeah."

"Not really," he said, and sighed, as if I had missed something important. "You don't see a face with it. There's no name associated with it."

At 11 o'clock, the doors opened and surgeons began to make their way over to the tables. Perna had partitioned off half the room for a group of gynecologists. There were nine new stations with female torsos. The women were covered in plastic, except for their vaginas, which had been propped up on blocks like small ruddy mountains.

It is a rare woman who would expose herself in this way to strangers—let alone in a banquet hall—and even the surgeons seemed uncomfortable.

"I don't want to know what's going on over there," one of the urology instructors told me as he put on his gloves. "I mean, a kidney is a kidney, but a vagina is human."

Dr. Kenneth Rutledge, a soft-spoken urologist who had flown in from Atlanta for the course, stood nearby. Before he reached through the Lap Disc opening into a torso, he put four gloves on his hand.

"We're risking ourselves here," he told me later, "because we don't know if some of these people may have died from HIV."

He looked at the torso, and his expression crumbled.

"Oh, this is gross," he said. "This is worse than a horror movie." He looked up at me. "I'm amazed that you, as a nonmedical person, can be in here and not be vomiting."

It was a good point. I decided to head for the ocean.

To get to the beach at the Trump, you have to walk down three flights of whitewashed concrete stairs at the back of the hotel. Even after Trump's big investment, it feels like the entrance to a municipal swimming pool. The metal railing beside the stairs was hot beneath my hand. The sun beat down, but I couldn't get rid of the chills. I was wearing a heavy wool pantsuit and a long-sleeved shirt, but my teeth were chattering.

I thought: *Get out on the warm beach with live people. Shake off all this death.* When I reached the bottom of the stairs, I turned the corner and there before me were dozens of torsos: white fleshy torsos, walnut-colored torsos in bikinis, hot sweaty torsos on towels in the sand.

I stood for a moment on the concrete landing, feeling the heat through the rubber soles of my shoes. If Allen Tyler cut off the heads and limbs of these bodies on the beach, they'd look a lot like the ones upstairs. Fresh torsos are like that. They look and feel real, which is precisely what makes them so valuable.

In 1789, a writer named Francis Hopkinson published a poem entitled "An Oration, Which Might Have Been Delivered to the Students in Anatomy." The poem contains the lines:

> No *where's the difference?—to th' impartial eye*
> *A leg of mutton and a human thigh*
> *Are just the same—for surely all must own*
> *Flesh is but flesh, and bone is only bone.*

In the poem, Hopkinson defends the practice of anatomical dissection and points to something that I was quickly learning: When your livelihood depends on dead bodies, it helps to think of them as something else. In the funeral industry, that something else is very often meat.

I've talked to many people in the funeral business—funeral directors who spoke in melancholy whispers, members of the local Lions Club, brassy salesman types, and guys who carried guns with them when they picked up a body, "just in case." When it came to questions of human flesh, the analogies they offered were much the same.

"How long can a fresh body last in a van?" I asked one man.

"You ever put a steak out in the sun?"

"How hard is it to cut one up?" I asked another.

"It's like carving a turkey. If someone wants a drumstick, you better know where the joints are. If you've got a sharp knife, it ain't hard."

"Can you freeze a corpse?"

"Just like a chicken."

A veteran New York City cop who has coped with dead bodies found everywhere—from suitcases to trash cans—put it most succinctly: "You don't think about what it was. You think about what it is. And it's a lump of meat."

Upstairs in my room at the Trump later that evening, I ran water for a bath and set about making coffee. As I spooned creamer into my cup, I suddenly detected the smell of decomposing flesh. I sniffed the white powder. Yes, there it was. But it was everywhere. In the coffee beans. Out on the balcony. Was it me?

I took off my clothes, avoiding the enormous mirror on the closet door, and slid into the tub. The hard porcelain rubbed painfully against my bones, and I realized, looking down, that in two days I had dropped at least five or six pounds. My stomach was sunk below my ribs, my arms floated like the branches of a sapling, and I could smell the foul odor of death wafting up from the warm water. I stuck my nose into a bottle of the Trump's green sea-grass aroma-therapy bath gel until the gooey liquid was touching my nostrils, but the nauseatingly sweet smell only intensified. (Olfactory hallucinations, I later learned, are very often associated with psychological conditions, and it is common for people who experience them to believe that they them-selves are the cause of the odors.)

———

As I lay in the tub, my fear mounting, I remembered a con-versation that I had had with Richard Santore, a retired funeral director from Brooklyn, who sought to be known in the 1980s as the "Crazy Eddie of the Funeral Business." Santore was one of the first people in the funeral industry, as far as I can tell, to start his own donor program. In the 1970s, he founded the Anatomical Gift Bank of New York, which shared offices with his funeral home, and which was later investigated by the Health Department for not obtain-ing and filing the proper paperwork for donated bodies. In 1979, five of his cadavers went missing and were discovered in a warehouse in Florence, Kentucky. But Santore contin-ued to receive bodies until the 1980s.

When I mentioned this incident to him over the phone, Santore became agitated and told me to turn off the tape recorder. Later, he suggested that I stop concentrating on the past. "Just because Charlie Jones did something terribly wrong five years ago, is it right to rehash it today in such a way that it makes it appear as though I do it as a regular practice? That's wrong. That's yellow journalism," he told me from his new office in Tennessee, where he published a now-defunct online newsletter titled *Today in Deathcare*. I asked him, if he ever got up to New York, whether he'd like to meet me and talk in person.

"Yes," he said. "And maybe I'll strangle you."

After we hung up, Santore called me at two in the morning. His number showed up on my caller ID. When I picked up the phone, there was no answer, but I could hear the caller breathing heavily on the other end of the line.

"Hello? Hello?" I said.

After I got out of the bathtub, a feeling akin to defiance compelled me to call room service and order a rare hamburger. When it arrived, I sat down on the bed and ate the bloody meat in my underwear.

———

As the weekend dragged on, the smell of death in the Ocean Room grew stronger and stronger until it was unbearable. Charloff, the assistant, was angry.

He said, "I told the guy from the hotel at the beginning, that if you keep it cold in here, there will be no smell. If you don't, there's nothing we can do."

During nearly ten hours of torso work, the doctors had successfully performed nephrectomies, both hand-assisted and laparoscopic; some had even removed the prostate laparscopically, an incredibly challenging operation. They had learned how to sew and cut and cauterize tissue, manipulating their instruments through minute incisions.

Perna was delighted by their progress. He said the next thing he was going to do was expand into gastric-bypass surgery, also known as stomach stapling, a "very upcoming field." Perna said that 65 percent of people in the United States are overweight, with the fastest-growing obesity rate among children.

"Augie is really a very bright man," Charloff said later. "He really is. He's a thinker when it comes to business."

"Now, the three of us, we want to get the bodies for ourselves," Charloff confided. "You have to do some market research . . . go to hospitals."

Listening to Charloff, I was reminded of Michael Brown. Charloff seemed like an unlikely candidate to run his own body-parts company. He was simple and not at all dark, the sort of guy who likes to drink a beer and sit out on his back porch in the evening, watching the stars and playing with his dog.

"Augie pretty much will have to direct me as far as how to sell the product," Charloff went on. "How to say the right things to the people and how not to make people think that I'm a bad guy because I don't know the lingo, so to speak. That's where Augie comes in."

"I feel like I'm witnessing something revolutionary," I said, half in disbelief.

"You are! You know why?" Charloff looked at me and grinned. Then he explained to me that he had called officials in Pennsylvania and Florida to discuss the legalities of the tissue-banking business and they had no idea what he was talking about. "So that means I've got to be one of the first hundred or less that's doing something like this, and you know, I don't mean to sound coarse, but that's a nice living."

Charloff nodded toward the torsos and laughed. "And it's not like you're selling cars, because what you're doing is you're bettering mankind."

I asked him about the shaky legality of profiting from corpses.

Charloff smiled and said, "We're not selling these. They're being leased." Then he laughed. In fact, Perna has the remains cremated when he is done with them. Then he either returns the ashes to the supplier, which returns them to the families of the deceased, or he simply has the crematorium scatter them to the winds.

———

After I got home from the conference, I met up with Perna at a diner near his house in New Jersey. He was wearing a tight black T-shirt, jeans, and cowboy boots. He looked smaller without his surgical scrubs. His cell phone rang throughout our conversation. The first time, it was his mother. "Hi, Ma," he said, exasperated. "Yes, Ma." Covering up the mouthpiece he whispered, "I take care of my parents, too." And then he hung up the phone.

A few minutes later, his second wife, April Malloy Perna, called from North Carolina, where she had moved after filing for divorce. Malloy runs a babysitting company called Emergency Nanny Care Services, which Perna funded. "She's the one you should be doing a story on, not me," Perna said. "Child care in America is the worst in the country." From Perna's tone on the phone, it appeared that the two were still very much together. "The business is booming," he said proudly. Indeed, the company was doing so well that after just six months in business, its Web site announced, it was expanding into "care for the elderly."

When I asked Perna about his own plans for the future, he told me that he was moving forward with his idea to start a tissue bank. "The donor side is the place to be," Perna said. "You know, when I first started this, man, I could've gotten eighty a week. Torsos were being destroyed! They were taking spines out of them. They were using their heads for dentistry and plastic surgery, and it was like, *the torso*, who wants it?" Now tissue banks can't keep up with the demand. "If you want a shoulder, we're talking ninety days at least!" he said, giggling. "That's where the money is!" He picked up his fork and began slapping the back of the tines against his palm. "Oh, shoulders! Knees!"

What about the bodies? I asked. How will you find them?

"Mostly in nursing homes," he said. "Funeral homes. People that can't afford to get buried."

Unfortunately, a dead person is much more difficult to commodify than a live pig. Still, you can approximate a pig farm by choosing the right location. Florida, for example, would be perfect, Perna reasoned, except that it has too many rich people, who tend not to be impressed by any dollar-dangling. *Give me your tired, your poor*, I thought.

The wretched refuse of your teeming shore. Send these, the homeless, tempest-tossed, to me.

As Perna sees it, there are plenty of people who would like to make something of themselves in death, if not in life. He imagines a streamlined future for the cadaver trade, in which straight talk about real needs replaces prudish euphemism. "If I was you," he said, "I would open up a company that is just going to basically buy bodies." The company would pay, he said, something like $20,000 for a cadaver, chop it up, and then sell the pieces for $200,000. Poor families would enjoy a new source of income, the company would make a large profit, and the marketplace would finally be provided precisely the parts it desired.

"You wanna buy a heart?" he asked. "Here it is, baby! One through ten! Different sizes! Different blood types! Whatever! Think about it," he said. "It would be like farming. You'd be farming people."

"Okay, ma'am," he said, adopting an official tone. "You have a good liver. You have a good this and that. Sign up and we're going to put a band in your butt. We're going to monitor you twenty-four hours a day. And as soon as you die, you're mine."

———

Augie Perna is not the first person to have seen a future in corpses. For centuries, men have made their livings tramping through the dark chambers of death and turning over the flesh and bones of their brothers for cash.

chapter 5

The Resurrection Men

On a moonless night in December 1811, Joseph Naples rose from his rumpled bed with a hangover, threw on his clay-stained uniform, grabbed a large shovel and a crowbar, and headed out into the cold.

It was three in the morning, and the streets of London were damp and nearly deserted, but for a few sleepy beggars and drunken prostitutes. A slight, nimble man, Naples scurried through the narrow, muddy alleys, stepping around the piles of horse manure like a small animal hunting its prey. He stopped at the iron gates of a graveyard and was soon joined by a group of sinister men. Like Naples, the others were dressed in dirt-caked clothing that stank of rotting flesh.

Presently, a watchman appeared in the fog. He nodded to the men, swung open the heavy iron gate, and closed it behind them. He pointed out the new graves. Working

97

quickly and quietly, the men threw the damp, icy soil expertly over their shoulders so that it fell in a small, neat pile.

Working a grave was a delicate endeavor. The men had to be careful to avoid any rocks or gravel, lest the clank of their shovels attract the attention of a passing constable, a hungry watchdog, or an early-rising neighbor. Naples knew that within an hour or two, smoke would be rising from breakfast chimneys within sight of where he stood.

When at last they reached the coffin, Naples inserted a crowbar and pried off the lid. Eagerly, the men peered down to inspect their prize.

This moment was full of unpleasant surprises. One never knew what lay beneath the wormy soil: bodies jaundiced or eaten by maggots and half-rotted, or covered in festering smallpox boils. In that case, an angry call went out: "Thing's bad!"

But if the corpse was fresh, the men rejoiced and hauled it out of the dirt, removed its sacred white shroud, and stuffed it back in the coffin. Then they replaced everything as it was. They filled in the hole and smoothed over the dirt, taking care to arrange each stone as they had found it. Then they wrapped up the body like a trussed fowl, put it in a sack, and loaded it onto a wagon parked discreetly nearby.

This particular December night, Naples was lucky. "Got three," he noted laconically in his diary the next morning.

The Borough Gang, as these men were known, were the forefathers of modern-day body brokers, part of an underground network of entrepreneurs that supplied nineteenth-century British surgeons with corpses. At the time, the only bodies that could be legally dissected were those of hanged murderers. There weren't enough murderers to go around and so the surgeons depended on gangs of so-called resurrectionists, to supply them with "subjects."

The resurrection business was a lot like the cadaver trade today. It developed for similar reasons, employed the same kind of people, who used some of the same methods, and supplied the same sort of ambitious surgeons, who, like many surgeons today, were more concerned with their own education and professional advancement than with the provenance of their corpses. As long as they got them on time and in good order, that was enough.

The word surgery comes from the Greek *cheirourgia,* which means, literally, hand work. The Greeks learned surgery from the ancient Egyptians, who performed elective operations like circumcision and even a form of plastic surgery, which they employed to heal battle wounds. The Greeks learned to tie arteries to stop bleeding. In the sixth century B.C., medical schools proliferated in what is now modern Turkey and on the island of Cos, producing such medical giants as Hippocrates, whose writings provide detailed case histories and treatments for fractures and hemorrhoids. One hundred and fifty years after Hippocrates' death, in the fourth century B.C., a medical school in Alexandria, hosted dissection courses using the bodies of condemned criminals. Thanks to these courses, the famous surgeon Herophilos established the human brain as the center of consciousness and named the prostate.

Sadly, in the Middle Ages much of the medical knowledge advanced by the Greeks and then Romans was lost. Papal law prohibited human dissection, and the human body came to be seen merely as a source of mysterious ailments. Though pockets of medical study persisted throughout the Arab world and in southern Italy, many medical schools closed down. If someone became sick, it was God's wrath. If someone healed, it was a miracle. Knowing little of human anatomy, doctors abandoned the practice of tying blood vessels to control bleeding. Instead, they poured boiling oil or applied hot coils to the wounds of their patients.

But the Renaissance brought a renewed interest in medicine and specifically in human anatomy. In the sixteenth century, the Papal ban on dissection was finally lifted. In that same century, Andreas Vesalius performed dissections on corpses in Italy, which attracted students from all over Europe. Vesalius hired a famous artist to create woodcuts of his dissections and then published the illustrations in the now-famous anatomical text, *De Humani Corporis Fabrica* (The Structure of the Human Body). In his book, Vesalius corrected many of the misconceptions of the time, providing a detailed description of little-understood organs like the liver and the heart.

Despite their knowledge of human anatomy, surgeons still worked with considerable limitations. There was no reliable form of anesthesia, no understanding of bacteria or infection. Surgeons performed operations on tables while their patients sipped wine to forget the pain. Understandably, these operations were done only in cases of mortal danger. Unlike today, surgeons mostly treated surface wounds, amputated limbs, healed fractures, and removed superficial tumors.

By the late 1780s, dissection courses were being held in Vienna, Paris, as well as in London. In London, despite the growing need for corpses, there was no plentiful supply. Thus arose the resurrectionists.

Just as many body brokers today begin as funeral directors, as crematorium operators, or as dieners at medical schools, resurrectionists first worked as grave diggers and cemetery caretakers. Naples, for example, worked as a grave digger at Spa Fields Cemetery in London before joining the Borough Gang. Unlike his cronies, he came from a respectable family—his father had been a bookbinder. He was well-mannered and polite. But he was soon corrupted by the resurrectionists and their money.

A Scotsman named White introduced Naples to body snatching. White worked as a middleman, employing grave diggers to get him bodies and then selling them to gangs, who resold them to surgeons. One day, he enticed Naples to dig up a body or two and to procure for him some "canines," or teeth. Corpse teeth were valuable—the material of choice for dentures of the day. A timid, hardworking man, Naples did as he was told and White rewarded him for his work.

When he saw the money that could be made, Naples began to spend some of his night hours digging up bodies, and eventually he began robbing corpses full-time. A year or so later, he sold a body to White, who was stopped by a constable, and Naples was sentenced to two years in jail. He managed to escape but was unable to find work. So he joined the Borough Gang. For the next several years, he spent his days looking out for funerals and his nights digging up flesh.

Naples kept a diary of his job that was later published as *The Diary of a Resurrectionist*. He made his notations in a sloping scrawl in a ledger book and titled them, simply, "remarks." In the same way that a broker of today might call bodies "products," Naples refers to them as "things." He notes their size—"Large," "Large small," "Small," "Foetus"—their condition, and their price.

Monday October 5, 1812 Went to look out at different places, at night party went to Lamb [a cemetery] got 2 adults and 9 small took the whole to the Borough [hospital].

Monday October 19th Went to Lamb, got 1 Adult M. [opened another whole but bad with the small pox] took the above M. to Barth. [Bartholomew's hospital] came home . . .

Tuesday October 20th Went to Barthol. Bill had got pd. for the above Male I borrowed of him £1.10.0

[one pound ten shillings] went to Lamb came home at night met at the White [a pub] Hollis myself Jack & Tom Light, Bill not with us could not find his clothes: went to Lamb two adults M. took to Barthol. Butler again not with us came home.

Naples is matter-of-fact about his gruesome job. But that's not to say that it didn't affect him. He and the gang were often ill after handling a corpse, and they escaped the ghastly work by drinking. On the nights that they didn't "go out," they went to one of their favorite pubs to guzzle ale and "settle up the accounts."

Presiding over these evenings was their leader, Ben Crouch—or "Uncle Crouch," as the anatomy students called him. A tall man with coarse features and a pockmarked face, Crouch was an amateur boxer and a cunning businessman. While the gang got drunk, he counted the money and made sure, when he passed out the spoils, to stiff each and every one of them. By that point, the boys were usually too drunk to notice.

Crouch could be charming when necessary. At the beginning of each academic term, he went around to the medical schools to negotiate the rates. Dressed like a dandy, fobs hanging from his watch chain, he bustled around the dissecting room, bowing to the lecturers and winking at the dieners. But if he didn't get the price he wanted, he quickly became rude and abusive.

One of Crouch's regular customers was Dr. Astley

Cooper, a well-known surgeon and professor of anatomy at St. Thomas's Hospital. Surgeons like Cooper knew well where and how the resurrectionists got their bodies. But the unspoken rules of the body trade forbade him to ask any but the most general questions of his ne'er-do-well procurers. Graveyard clay might be caked on their uniforms, but nothing would be said of the graveyard. A wink and a nod and full payment were enough, and the gang members were on their way.

Cooper openly despised the resurrectionists and referred to them as the "lowest dregs of degradation," but he was a generous and very loyal client nonetheless. His success depended on them.

Every morning at six, Cooper rose and disappeared into the shed behind his house, which he used as a dissection room. There he experimented until breakfast on a variety of carcasses. Cooper would dissect anything he could get his hands on—not simply human corpses, but fish, chicken, stray mutts enticed to their death by his servant, and even, on one occasion, a massive dead elephant, provided by his friends at the London Zoo. He once boasted, "There is no person, let his situation in life be what it may, whom, if I were disposed to dissect, I could not obtain."

Like Perna's course in Florida, these morning sessions gave Dr. Cooper the chance to practice his techniques and to experiment with new ones. As a result, Cooper became one of the great innovators of his time. He was the first surgeon to tie the carotid artery for an aneurysm and the first to amputate a leg at the hip. This last operation required him to tie four blood vessels, all while his patient was awake, sipping wine. Later, King George IV handpicked Cooper to remove a tumor from his head, a difficult operation even by today's standards, but which was a great success.

After a bit of tea and breakfast, Cooper saw patients in his home. At lunchtime, he hurried to Guy's Hospital, where he made rounds, lectured to students, and performed dissections in the amphitheater. By seven, he was home for a quick dinner and then set out to see more patients or to teach another class.

When he finally crawled into bed, Dr. Cooper was often awoken by a knock at the door. There, standing in the moonlight, would be one of the resurrectionists, claiming he'd found some fresh grave to work but needed an advance to bribe the grave digger or the watchman. Always eager for more specimens, Cooper handed over the money, never suspecting that the gang had tricked him and taken the bodies to another school where they got twice the price. Cooper and his suppliers often fought about money.

Wednesday, January 22, 1812 At 4 o'clock in the morning got up, Bill & me went to the Hospital Crib and [got] 1 for Mr. Cooper's Lectures, had a dispute with the party, at home all night. Ben got drunk.

Successful gangs fiercely guarded their territory, and if they found interlopers trying to poach their corpses or customers, they quickly squashed them. Perhaps a friendly trip to the constable to turn in the miscreants. Perhaps a visit to the anatomy lab for some dissection of their own. The point was to render their rivals' bodies useless for dissection.

On Monday, August 24, 1812, when the Borough Gang ran into a group of their competitors, a Jewish gang of body snatchers run by Israel Chapman, they followed them through town until they "lost scent." But when they learned that Chapman had got a "Male," they made an appointment to settle the score and had a "row."

Anatomy instructors learned to keep quiet about these battles. The resurrectionists had the upper hand. If the professors spoke out, they risked seeing their supply of corpses abruptly dry up—or even seeing corpses that had been bought and paid for disappear. In fact, rather than hold the resurrectionists accountable, surgeons were more likely to appease them.

When the gang members were arrested, Cooper had them freed. When they were locked up, he supported their families. When he sent them into the countryside to pick up the body of someone who had died of an interesting ailment, he paid for their coach, their lodging, and food expenses, as well as for the cost of the bodies themselves.

In 1828, Dr. Cooper spent nearly a hundred pounds keeping the resurrectionists in business. The reason for this was simple, he later said: "I would not remain in the room with a man who attempted to perform an operation in surgery, who was unacquainted with anatomy, unless he would be directed by others; he must mangle the living if he has not operated on the dead."

The London constables were equally circumspect. Though British law strictly forbade grave robbing, and constables made a show of disapproval, they were partial to the doctors, fearing that if they cracked down too hard on the resurrectionists, the medical students wouldn't be properly trained, since the number of executed bodies made available every year for study didn't begin to meet the needs of the medical schools.*

They had a good reason to protect the interests of the doctors and medical students. In 1803, England had plunged into a major war with France, and those who fought the forces of Napoleon Bonaparte had learned to expect massive casualties. The lives of thousands of brave British soldiers depended on the skill of military surgeons at the battlefront.

_____

More than a decade after the Borough Gang got started in London, two men in Edinburgh conceived of a far more sinister plan to procure corpses.

William Hare managed a grim lodging house in an Edinburgh slum: three ramshackle rooms with a pigsty in the back. The lodgers were the usual sad assortment found at

* By one estimate, between 1805 and 1820, roughly seventy-seven criminals were executed every year in Great Britain. Meanwhile, the medical students in London numbered over a thousand, with almost as many in Edinburgh in need of cadavers to dissect.

such places: They were often poor, often destitute. Many were sick and couldn't afford a proper doctor. A few hoped desperately to better themselves, but many had simply given up.

One day, a man named William Burke checked into the lodging house accompanied by his wife, a woman named Helen M'Dougal.

An industrious man who had a weakness for drink, Burke earned his money hawking old clothes and skins while he and his woman moved from lodging house to lodging house. Hare took a liking to his new lodger and let Burke set up shop in a small side room. There, Burke began mending old shoes that he'd found on the street, which he later resold. Burke and Hare became friends and drinking partners, often tipping back spirits late into the night.

Their sinister enterprise began innocently enough. One of Hare's lodgers, a lonely old man named Desmond, had fallen ill with dropsy. His body swelled. His face and stomach grew bloated, and he died—still owing four pounds in rent.

William Hare discovered the corpse. He might be forgiven for seeing the death of his lodger primarily as a case of lost income for himself. Bitter at this turn of events, Hare and William Burke decided to drag the old lodger's corpse over to a hospital and recoup the debt. The two men bundled up the lodger's body and lugged it through the streets to Surgeon's Square, the headquarters of Dr. Knox, who was then a well-known surgeon and teacher of anatomy. Dr. Knox rewarded Hare and Burke handsomely for the old man's corpse, paying them a little more than seven pounds in cash.

Before they left, Dr. Knox encouraged the men to bring him other corpses. They realized then just how much more a man was worth dead than alive.

But rather than go to the trouble of digging up corpses in the overcrowded, stinking cemeteries of Edinburgh, Burke and Hare opted for a more convenient approach: murder. They certainly didn't have to go far to find a victim—there were plenty of potential corpses right there at the lodging house.

Burke and Hare's first victim was a miller named Joseph. Like Desmond, Joseph had become ill while living at the lodging house. Though weak, he still eagerly accepted when Hare invited him in for a friendly chat and a few generous glasses of stout.

Knowing that a violent method of murder would be detected by the doctors, Burke and Hare waited until Joseph grew sleepy, then lowered a pillow over his nose and mouth and smothered him to death. When they were sure he was dead, they stripped Joseph of his clothes, packed up his naked body, and hauled it over to the offices of Dr. Knox, where it was received without any compunction. This time they earned ten pounds.

And so it went for one whole year. During that time, Burke and Hare asphyxiated sixteen people—many of them old women—and sold all sixteen bodies to Dr. Knox. The doctor seems never to have raised the obvious question: How did Burke and Hare happen to know so many people who had suddenly died?

Their killing spree would almost certainly have continued—but, like many men in their position, the two friends got carried away by their success and grew careless. Alerted by Burke's suspicious behavior, one of Hare's female lodgers did some exploring in Burke's bedroom and discovered a corpse hidden in the corner under some straw.

The woman told her husband about the corpse, and her husband confronted Mrs. Burke. As he later recalled, "I asked what it was that she had in the house; and she said, 'What was it?' And I said, 'I suppose you know very well what it is.'"

Mrs. Burke fell on her knees and begged him not to tell anyone about the body upstairs. But he would have none of it and promptly informed the police.

When word of the murders got out, all of Edinburgh was in an uproar. There were rumors that Dr. Knox had ordered Burke and Hare to kill their victims. How else, people whispered, could two such ignorant men devise such a foolproof method? Word spread that they had killed as many as thirty-two people, that Knox was in on all of the crimes, and that he'd helped conceal the identities of the corpses. If he wasn't guilty, why hadn't he questioned the steady stream of bodies that Burke and Hare delivered when it was clear that none of the bodies had ever been interred?

There was no evidence that Knox knew about the murders, and he was never prosecuted, but an investigative panel later reprimanded him for not making inquiries about the origin of the corpses. Testifying as a witness for the prosecution, Hare managed to get immunity. Thanks to his testimony, William Burke was found guilty. After a sensational trial, he was hanged in front of nearly 25,000 jeering spectators. His body was then turned over to anatomy students for dissection.

In 1832, partly as a result of the Burke and Hare murders, the British government passed the Anatomy Act, which was intended to put an end to the cadaver trade in England once and for all. The new law provided surgeons with the "unclaimed" bodies of the poor and friendless for dissection.

———

Meanwhile, across the ocean in America, resurrectionists—or "ghouls" as they were known in the press—were doing a thriving business. While less well known today than its counterpart in England, the American body-snatching business grew into a large and complex enterprise that lasted well into the twentieth century.* In 1921, the diener at Vanderbilt University School of Medicine was still buying bodies from a ghoul.

Until the late eighteenth century, there were few skilled doctors and even fewer surgeons in America. Doctors who tended to the sick in Colonial times were often little more than interested laymen who did the best that they could, prescribing remedies of dubious value like bloodletting and vomiting. In the absence of proper medical schools, the distinction between a trained physician and a quack was vague at best.

* Michael Suppol has written a remarkable account of this early cadaver trade in his book *A Traffic of Corpses*.

Ambitious medical students who could afford the journey visited London and studied under famous professors like John and William Hunter. As they returned from their travels and disseminated what they had learned, an interest in anatomy started to take hold in America—in particular in cities like Boston, Philadelphia, and New York. According to Michael Sappol, author of *A Traffic of Dead Bodies*, between 1810 and 1860, the number of medical schools in the United States increased from just five to sixty-five.

Courses in human dissection had a profound effect on the way in which doctors analyzed the ailments of their patients. For example, Dr. Ephraim McDowell, a surgeon in Kentucky, knew enough from dissecting a corpse to recognize that one of his patients, who claimed to be pregnant, was carrying not a child but an ovarian tumor. Realizing that this woman was in mortal danger, McDowell operated on her at his kitchen table and removed a twenty-two-pound tumor. Within a month, the woman had fully recovered.

By the mid-nineteenth century, all over the country, surgeons and their students were engaged in anatomy courses at medical schools, for which no corpse was spared. These schools, however, bore little resemblance to the medical schools of today. Many of them offered little more than cadavers and a lone instructor, and they were haphazardly run, driven more by commercial values than educational ones. Some were hosted by enterprising surgeons or simply by entrepreneurs who set up the corpses in their basements or attics and allowed aspiring surgeons to dissect them.

Because their main focus was anatomical dissection, the schools were particularly dependent on the availability of corpses and, therefore, on ghouls. Like England, America had no willed-body programs. To dismember a corpse on a table in a room full of strangers was a foreign and barbaric concept, and a punishment in the eyes of the public at the time. Worse, in most states, hanged criminals weren't available for dissection either. If medical schools wanted a steady source of corpses, they had to find someone who was willing to do the very dirty work of supplying them.

In the early days of body snatching in America, ghouls limited their activities to local graveyards, since they traveled by horse and wagon and had to have enough time to bring the corpses back to the medical schools before sunrise. Later, the advent of railroads allowed them to travel farther afield to collect corpses.

Train travel made it possible for them to ship large batches of corpses from state to state, any time of the day or night. In the process, they developed a spiderweb of shipping hubs, informants, and anatomist clients, which in many cases extended hundreds of miles. Small companies popped up to negotiate these shipments, finding reliable suppliers, buying the corpses, packing them up, and getting them to out-of-state clients.

The brokers and ghouls devised clever ways of disguising and preserving their "goods" for the journey. One method was to "pickle" the corpses in brine—likely a combination of salt and vinegar—and to pack them in wooden casks.

To procure corpses, the ghouls used a method similar to the one used by their counterparts in England. Like the Borough Gang, they traveled in groups. Typically, they carried with them a spade, a keyhole saw, and a piece of rope. In 1878, the *New York Times* featured this description from a Kentucky grave robber, who had described it to a local reporter from the *Courier Journal*:

On arriving at the grave, the spade is first called into use. One-half of the grave is marked off, and the dirt from the upper half of the coffin is thrown out. This work can be performed by a professional in about eight minutes. At this point, the saw comes into use. The saw is started into one edge of the coffin, and soon, with a noise resembling sobs and groans, has cut through the upper board, and often through the shroud and flesh of the subject! The further work of opening the coffin is easily performed. The manipulator of the saw raises his body with a hand on either side of the grave, a foot above the coffin's lid, and, loosening his hold upon either side, precipitates his whole weight upon the lid, which gives way with a crash.

Some body snatchers preferred a more delicate approach; rather than saw through the coffin lid and risk damaging the flesh of their prize, they drilled a line of holes across the top of the coffin. On occasion, a coffin would be fitted with a glass lid, which was easier to break than wood and made the body snatcher's job simpler. In any case, the ghoul removed the lid and lowered a rope down to his assistant. The rope, which had a slipknot or a metal hook at the end, was thrown around the head of the corpse and word was given to the man up above to "hoist away."

This method of retrieval did not always proceed smoothly. "I remember once that the whole head of a woman whose neck we tied the rope around came off in our grasp," the resurrectionist told the *Courier Journal* reporter. Once the corpse was out of the grave, the men would "double up the body 'nose and knee like' and dump it in a sack, put it in a wagon, and come to town."

Clues to a good corpse could be had for a fee. It was customary in some parts of the country for the undertaker to leave a piece of coal at the site of a particularly auspicious grave. The undertaker, in turn, received a portion of the body snatcher's profits. Other informants included the minister, who, having led the funeral service, was familiar with the burial site, the caretaker of the cemetery, and the grave digger.

The ghouls' victims were almost always poor men, since male cadavers had better musculature. They were also often black. Partly, this was a matter of convenience. It was customary in some cities to bury poor people and African Americans next to each other, or in neighboring cemeteries. The poor were often interred naked, without coffins, sometimes in mass graves, which made them very easy to steal.

Mostly, though, the reason was simply prejudice. According to the book *Bones in the Basement: Post-Mortem Racism* *in Nineteenth Century Medical Training,* in 1831, the Medical College of South Carolina "advertised in a circular that it obtained 'subjects . . . for every purpose' from the African American population rather than the white population of Charleston so that they could carry out 'proper dissections . . . without offending any individuals.'"*

More than forty years after England put an end to body snatching, the body business was thriving in America. In 1878, according to Michael Sappol's research, at least twelve body snatchings made the newspapers, and there were likely many more that were never reported. Citizens lived in terror that their bodies or the bodies of their loved ones would be stolen. They hired watchmen to safeguard the coffins, buried their family members in "mortsafes," which were metal cages that enclosed the coffins, and invested in all kinds of other creative gizmos marketed by opportunistic undertakers.

One gadget popular in Indiana was the "grave torpedo." The torpedo consisted of a simple spring attached to an iron cup containing explosive powder. If a body snatcher disturbed the dirt over a coffin, his movements would activate the spring, an explosion would result, and the dirt would be

---

* The authors of the book show that blacks were targeted more frequently than whites in other areas of the South as well. Professors Robert L. Blakely and Judith Harrington examined the bones that had been buried in the basement of the Medical College of Georgia between 1840 and 1880. Seventy-nine percent of the bodies they found belonged to African Americans, despite the fact that blacks accounted for only 37 to 47 percent of the population in Augusta at that time.

thrown up in the ghoul's face. How successful this was in deterring the body snatchers is unclear.

The protests of the public did little to curb the body trade. As long as there was demand for specimens, there were ghouls skulking in the cemeteries. When states made it a crime to steal bodies, the price of corpses rose, but the surgeons and medical students continued to buy from the ghouls. They claimed to have no choice. One anatomist in Michigan complained that he needed as many as ninety to a hundred bodies every year. "In order to meet this enormous demand, I have labored early and late and have tested every honorable method," he said, but in the end he fell back on "other means."

No corpse was safe from the ghouls. In May 1878, congressman John Scott Harrison died suddenly in North Bend, Ohio. News of the congressman's death attracted a lot of attention. He was a wealthy man, the son of a former U.S. president, which made him a near celebrity in that era, and consequently his corpse was the subject of keen interest. Surgeons would have been eager to study his brain, to examine his heart and its ventricles, to cut through his skin down to the bone, to dissect his arteries and veins.

Knowing this, and fearing that grave robbers would steal his body, Harrison's sons weren't about to take any chances. In addition to a coffin, they ordered a special cement vault for their father's body. The vault was to be covered up with a heavy stone and then the whole thing filled with rocks and logs. With a man so important, they couldn't be too cautious. They even arranged for a watchman to come and check on the grave every hour for a week after the funeral.

On the appointed day, after all of the security measures were in place, Harrison's friends and family gathered around his grave by the Ohio River to say good-bye. The ceremony proceeded smoothly until suddenly one of the mourners spotted a suspicious sign at a nearby plot. The dirt around the grave of a young boy had been disturbed—a telltale sign of a grave robbing. Sure enough, when they went to investigate the plot, the mourners turned up nothing but worms. It was just as they had feared: The boy's body had been stolen.

Outraged that anyone could be so brazen and unfeeling as to steal the body of a small child, and fearing that the same criminals might get to Harrison, the group wasted no time in organizing a search party. Led by Benjamin Harrison, the congressman's son, they headed straight for Cincinnati, which was then home to several medical schools. The police joined them, and by the next day they had obtained a search warrant for the Medical College of Ohio.

Finding no trace of the boy at the school, they were about to leave when one of them noticed a rope on a pulley leading down through a trapdoor in the floor. Curious, they decided to see what was on the other end. As they pulled on the rope, a naked male figure rose up slowly through the floor. The man's head had been wrapped in cloth. He was too large to be a boy, that was certain, but the mourners were intrigued. When they removed the cloth, much to their horror, there staring back at them was the pale face of Congressman Harrison.

Sure enough, when they went to investigate, they discovered that Harrison's grave had been dug into during the night and the glass cover of his coffin broken in pieces. The watchman, whom they had paid to keep the robbers away, had no explanation.

The police promptly arrested the medical school diener and charged him with concealing a stolen body. During their inquiries, they learned that the Miami Medical College, another Cincinnati medical school, was being used as a shipping hub by a local grave robber.

Dr. Henri Le Caron, who went by the alias Dr. Charles O. Morton, was a handsome and daring doctor who had worked his way through Detroit Medical College moonlighting as a ghoul. He had since become the head of a gang of body snatchers and was in the business of furnishing corpses from Ohio to the University of Michigan by way of the Miami Medical College. Once he had enough specimens for a shipment, he loaded them into barrels labeled "pickles" and sent them on to Michigan. When the Ohio police learned about his scheme, they rushed to Ann Arbor. Sure enough, there in the pickling vat of the morgue, where the corpses were preserved, was the body of the small boy who had been laid to rest next to Congressman Harrison.

In a letter to the *Cincinnati Times,* the Dean of the Faculty at the Ohio Medical College, Dr. Robert Bartholow, denied any knowledge of the Harrison theft. "A very great misconception seems to exist as regards the part taken by the Faculty and their assistants, in procuring the material for dissection," he wrote. "The men engaged in the business of procuring subjects are, of course, unknown to the Faculty. They bring the material to the college, receive the stipulated price, and disappear as mysteriously as they come."

Incensed, Benjamin Harrison wrote his own letter to the citizens of Cincinnati, which was published in the *New York Times*. "He charges the distinguished men who compose the Faculty of the Ohio College," the *Times* reported, "with shielding the guilty party from justice. The bodies brought to the college, he says, are purchased and paid for by an officer of the college. The body snatcher stands before him, and takes from his hand the fee for his hellish work. He is not an occasional visitant. He is often there, and it is silly to say he is unknown. 'Who did it, gentlemen of the Faculty? Who . . . hung him by the neck in the pit?'"

A grand jury later indicted Dr. Morton and J. Q. Marshall, the diener, but predictably no professor at either medical school was ever charged. Medical school faculties consistently escaped prosecution. But cases like the "Harrison Horror" eventually forced states to address the problem of grave robbing once and for all. The issue of how to obtain a sufficient quantity of corpses for dissection had been debated for years all over the country, but it wasn't always satisfactorily resolved.

In 1830, a special state committee in Massachusetts studied the problem of body snatching. Its members acknowledged that dissection was "an ultimate good for the future of medical science," without which "valuable lives would be lost." They even went so far as to ennoble anatomical dissection: "Who would not prefer, to be useful even after death to his survivors, rather than to fester and decay, to feed the numerous worms and to undergo the slow and disgusting process of chemical decomposition?"

The committee members would have had little luck convincing the American public. So they proposed legalizing the system that the anatomists and ghouls already had in place: "Why not legalize the dissection of those who died without family or friends? Those whose bodies would be unclaimed, are the vicious and depraved," they argued. "They shared the benefits, but bore none of the burdens of the social state and of civilization." This solution ensured that the "better" people would no longer have to worry about having their bodies snatched from their graves and the bodies of the "vicious" would repay their debt to society. "Can an intelligent legislator, divesting himself of prejudice, refuse to give this aid to the cause of science?"

So it was that the Massachusetts Anatomy Act passed in 1831. Eventually, every state would adopt similar laws designating unclaimed bodies, including the bodies of those people who died without family or friends in state-run institutions like prisons and insane asylums—and in some cases the very poor—for anatomical dissection. In 1947, Tennessee was the last state to pass such a law.

Laws about unclaimed bodies and the bodies of paupers

exist in most states today, but few Americans realize it, and only seven of the fifty states enforce these laws. In Maryland, whenever a person dies in a hospital and is not claimed within seventy-two hours, his body is shipped to the state anatomy board. Pennsylvania, Virginia, New York, Delaware, and Arkansas enforce similar laws.

Beginning in the 1950s, medical schools began to accept body donations from the public. The first state to legalize body donation was California. Dr. Horace Magoun, chair of the Anatomy Department at UCLA, pioneered the anatomical-gift program. In 1950, he convinced the California legislature to pass a law allowing citizens to donate their bodies for medical education.

Five years later, UCLA had enough bodies to meet its needs for thirty years. By 1968, every state in the union had passed some version of the Uniform Anatomical Gift Act. Through donations and unclaimed bodies, most schools were able to meet their needs. But that would change as the demand for flesh and bones grew once again.

Several factors fueled the underground cadaver trade of today. Between 1965 and 1980, the number of accredited medical schools in the United States grew from 88 to 126. Class sizes grew, too, so the number of doctors in training more than doubled. By the 1970s, medical school curricula were also expanding to include special education courses using cadaver parts for teaching in areas like emergency medicine and orthopedic anatomy.

Anatomy departments felt growing pressure. Some of

the pressure came from within medical programs. Some of it came from outside advocacy groups. In the late 1970s, associations like the American Academy of Orthopedic Surgeons began holding their own surgical-skills workshops. They, too, required cadavers and body parts. As surgical technology advanced, medical-device companies started hosting their own courses to showcase their wares. They, too, needed body parts. Bodies were being distributed in new ways, funneled out of medical schools, and in some cases from funeral homes, into a new underground trade.

chapter 6

"Brokered Sounds Bad, Doesn't It?"

On July 24, 1986, UPS workers at the Standiford Field Sorting Center in Louisville, Kentucky, were inspecting cargo for an overnight flight, when they spotted several boxes from Philadelphia marked "aerosol." UPS won't transport aerosol containers, so the workers pulled the boxes aside.

That's when they noticed a smell. It was sweet, overripe, like something that had spoiled. Meat perhaps? The boxes were also leaking. Better open them up, the workers thought.

Nestled inside were five human heads wrapped in plastic. They looked alive but for their severed necks, which oozed a rancid, bloody fluid. The workers were appalled.

Before long, the phones were ringing in the office of the local coroner, Dr. Richard Greathouse. Greathouse is a plainspoken southern doctor. He's seen plenty of strange cases in his twenty-nine years on the job, but this was one of the weirdest he'd seen yet. "Something really hokey was going on that boiled down to one thing," he said. "Somebody had murdered these people in Philly and was getting rid of the evidence." Greathouse called the Philadelphia Police Department.

Within hours, homicide detective Daniel Rosenstein had traced the boxes to a four-story Philadelphia mansion on a quiet, tree-lined street in the elegant neighborhood of Rittenhouse Square. The limestone mansion was home to Dr. Martin Spector, a well-known eye, ear, and nose doctor. Spector lived upstairs with his wife and used the bottom floors as his office.

Inside, in a second-floor refrigerator, Rosenstein and his partners found eight pairs of frozen ears. They also found an order for seventeen frozen arms and "half heads with brains," from a Boulder, Colorado, research institute. When they asked Spector about these parts, the elderly doctor conceded that he'd been shipping ears and heads around the country to doctors and researchers for about fifteen years. But he refused to name his source, other than to say he got the parts from a "pathologist's assistant."

Soon, other pieces of the story emerged. One of Spector's former secretaries claimed that a mysterious man in a white lab coat had delivered ears to the office in paper lunch bags. Sometimes, she said, he brought heads wrapped in plastic garbage bags. She said Spector told her to give the man cash as payment for the deliveries.

Spector's body business was a casual enterprise. While his patients thumbed through *People* magazine in the waiting room, his secretaries sat upstairs, packing arms, heads, and ears into boxes for the UPS man. During coffee breaks, they joked about the doctor's side business. There was the time his precious heads fell off a UPS truck and rolled down the street. That one always got a lot of laughs.

The story was horrific and strange, but the consensus in the Philadelphia medical community was that this was the work of one old, and very sick, man. While police continued to investigate, Dr. Edward J. Stemmler, who was then dean of the University of Pennsylvania School of Medicine, promised to review Dr. Spector's privileges at the hospital. Perhaps it was time Spector retired, said Stemmler.

Little did Stemmler know what was going on in the university's morgue. In a search of Spector's downtown office, detectives turned up the name of a University of Pennsylvania diener and those of several employees of other local medical schools, whom Spector admitted he had enticed to supply him with parts. The men stole the body parts from dismembered medical school cadavers and autopsied bodies in the morgue.

Soon, Lynwood Summers of the University of Pennsylvania Hospital was arrested after confessing that he'd been supplying Spector with stolen body parts for ten years, earning $150 per head, $65 per arm, and $20 for a set of ears. On some occasions, he said, he made as much as $2,000 in cash for just one delivery. Summers harvested the parts from corpses that had undergone autopsies at the hospital but weren't donors.

Wilbert Richardson, a diener at the University of Pennsylvania Medical School, was also arrested. Later, two other employees were implicated: Reuben Whitehead of Philadelphia VA Medical Center, and Lenard Stephen of Thomas Jefferson University Hospital. All of these men had sold body parts to Spector, who resold them to places like the Otologic Research Center in Denver, Colorado, where doctors used them to hone their surgery skills.

Unlike most states, Pennsylvania prohibits the exportation of body parts. The law also requires that anyone receiving a donated body have a license from the state, which Spector did not. The Philadelphia District Attorney charged the dieners and Spector with conspiracy, theft, receiving stolen property, abuse of a corpse, and violating the health code by shipping body parts out of the state. Spector lost his license to practice medicine. Summers, Richardson, and Whitehead were all fired.

The Philadelphia medical community was shocked by these further developments. "The medical center is deeply disturbed by the possibility that its carefully managed systems for the handling of human cadavers may have been violated," Dr. Stemmler told a reporter.

The medical schools trusted that the criminals had been punished and that these were isolated cases. Across America, there was little discussion of the scandal and its implications. But every medical school in the country should have taken notice. The Spector scandal was the first of many to come.

For the past twenty years, some medical schools have

exploited their generous donors over and over again. Inspired by the growing demand for parts, their employees have sold bodies for profit into the underground business without a second thought. In some cases, these "brokers" have been lowly dieners like the Pennsylvania men. But in others, professors have sanctioned the business, accepting donated bodies that they know they don't need and selling them to supplement their departmental budgets.

People who donate their bodies to medical schools rarely know anything about their final destination. The consent form they sign may well be vague, giving little if any information about how the body will be used, when, by whom, and for what purpose. Many of these donors are also very trusting, assuming that medical institutions and physicians will not betray them.

———

By the time Dr. Spector was arrested in Philadelphia, Arthur Rathburn had already been a diener at the University of Michigan Medical School for two years. A funeral director by trade, Rathburn is, according to those who know him, a tall man with an impressive mustache and a friendly demeanor. At the university, he was responsible for tagging corpses and setting them up for students. When necessary, he arranged for the shipment of corpses to other medical schools in need of bodies, and to brokers. Rathburn was the school's contact person, which may explain how he got the idea to become a broker himself.

Rathburn showed a lot of savvy in his approach to the cadaver trade. In 1987, he applied to join the American Association of Clinical Anatomists. The AACA had been founded in 1982 by a group of anatomical educators concerned that anatomy was losing favor in medical schools. With the rise of new technologies during the 1960s and 70s, medical school curricula had become more focused on microscope work in the labs. Even though the cadaver was the classic subject of anatomy, the new scientists were eager to shunt it aside.

The AACA wanted to promote the continued study of cadavers, which its members thought was crucial to a doctor's education. With this goal in mind, the association, which accepted professional members of all kinds—dental and medical school professors, as well as surgeons—extended its membership to dieners.

Arthur Rathburn submitted an impressive resume to the AACA, listing a degree from Western Michigan University and a stint at a coroner's office, which the secretary treasurer later discovered to be falsified. The AACA took Rathburn at his word, and he was quickly accepted.

In the meantime, Rathburn had started a business on the side supplying body parts. By 1990, he had been fired from his job at the university. The University of Michigan has instructed its employees not to talk about why Rathburn was dismissed. But a former administrator said that at the very least, he was commingling ashes of donated bodies. Rathburn's then assistant, Richard Lawson, confirmed this.

"He was burning more than one body at once. It was more expedient," Lawson explained. "We operated like we were moving product around a warehouse." Throughout my research into the cadaver trade, I left several messages for Rathburn, but never received a return phone call.

In Rathburn's defense, Lawson, who described his former boss as "good company," said the medical school administration was partly to blame for whatever may have happened since they exercised little oversight over the morgue. "There was nothing explicit that was made clear to me by the administration that you had to cremate one body at a time. If they wanted to be explicit about that, they could've come down to the morgue." As for Rathburn's side business, Lawson said that Rathburn had hired him after hours to help him transport bodies in one of Rathburn's vehicles to other locations. But Lawson saw nothing improper about this at the time. "I can't be accountable for the cash I was receiving. For all I knew it was something that was condoned by his supervisors."

In June 1990, Rathburn was fired from the university. The following year, Rathburn sued the school to prevent it from releasing any of his personnel files.

The AACA, having discovered that his credentials were falsified, expelled Rathburn from the association.

But Rathburn had no trouble staying in the business. Clients were easy to come by. As for the corpses, he simply contacted other medical schools. On October 8, 1990, he sent a letter to the Albert Einstein College of Medicine in

New York requesting body parts. His "requested needs" included 180 hands and wrists, 261 heads and necks, 250 skulls, 30 spines, and 240 feet. "Professional Mortuary Service assures each institution that any University or state requirements, rules and regulations will be explicitly adhered to," Rathburn promised in his letter to Dr. Peter Satir, the chairman of the Anatomy Department at Albert Einstein.

Satir didn't bite. But other schools were more than happy to supply Rathburn. In the mid-1990s, for example, Rathburn regularly bought bodies from the State University of New York in Syracuse. Between 1992 and 1999, the school billed Rathburn $159,435 for bodies and parts.

Arthur Rathburn now owns a successful body-brokerage company called International Biological, and in 2005 he paid nearly a million dollars for a crematorium in Richmond, Virginia. These days, he obtains corpses from a variety of suppliers, including a crematorium outside of Chicago, Anatomical Services, Inc., which he then supplies to the likes of Augie Perna's companies, the surgical equipment giant Medtronic, and to an assortment of plastic surgeons.

Rathburn's company is even licensed by the New York State Health Department. Every year, as required, Rathburn sends the department a report detailing his activities. In 2000, for example, he reported supplying thirty-one pairs of shoulders, fifteen pairs of feet, six pairs of knees, two pairs of hands, and five pairs of legs to two hospitals in New York, all of which he claimed were obtained in-house, from his own company, though Rathburn does not have a donor program. In 2002, by his own account Rathburn delivered forty-two heads and necks to the Marriott Marquis on Broadway. These, too, came from his company in Detroit.

Had the University of Michigan pursued a more rigorous, public investigation of Arthur Rathburn, it's possible that the information they uncovered about the trade in body parts would have forced them and any number of other medical schools to take steps to re-evaluate their programs.

But only one group of anatomists paid attention. In 1990, members of the AACA convened a special forum on the "Exploitation of Body Donor Programs." Among the thirty-odd people who met in Saskatoon, Saskatchewan, were Rathburn's former boss, Dr. William Burkel of the University of Michigan, Dr. Donald Cahill of the Mayo Clinic, and Dr. Andrew Payer of the University of Texas Medical Branch. Together they issued a cautionary memorandum about body-donor programs to their members. "Some programs," they noted, "appear to be exploited by individuals, groups and institutions. Of particular concern are independent entrepreneurs, acting as third-party brokers." In 1991, the anatomists formed a "special-interest group" and vowed to raise awareness about the problem.

Together with Dr. Donald Cahill, chair of the Anatomy Department at the Mayo Clinic, Dr. Andrew Payer began publishing a newsletter that was meant to serve as a forum for dieners and medical school faculty overseeing willed-body programs. In Volume 1, Number 1, an article co-authored by Dr. Cahill recommended that "cadaveric specimens be labeled in such a way that we know which participants, instructors, or investigators were working with each specimen. . . . Thus, if any untoward event occurred, tracking could be done to determine the association between participant, instructor, or investigator and cadaveric specimen." But it was difficult to get an audience. With the growing emphasis in anatomy departments on cellular biology, faculty and administrators were paying less and less attention to willed-body programs.

Many schools no longer even called their departments "Anatomy Departments." They were now departments of cellular biology. "They kept the bodies, but cared even less about how it was being run," Dr. Todd Olson, professor of anatomy at Albert Einstein, told me. "It was, you know, take your problems somewhere else. And, if you can bring in another $75,000 from the willed-body program so that we can use it for the general departmental fund, that would be great."

After three years, the newsletter died. History was bound to repeat itself. When it did, it happened right under Payer's nose.

In 1962, thirty-seven years before he met Michael Brown, Allen Tyler went to work at the University of Texas Medical Branch. His first job was in the cafeteria. Tyler was only sixteen then, but he was diligent and mature for his age, "like a little man," his best friend said. He always wore a jacket and a tie. When his friends went off to college, Tyler stayed behind and married his girlfriend, Rose, and they settled down in a bungalow in Galveston and had a baby girl. Like many ambitious people who never make it to college, Tyler was preoccupied with learning. Rose said, "He always wanted to engage with people that were above his level."

In 1965, Tyler moved up from the cafeteria and took a new job at the medical school working in the morgue. There, while he mopped the floors, he mixed with the doctors, whom he so much admired. Surgeons often dropped in to harvest specimens they needed for their courses. While they removed a pair of knees or shoulders from a corpse, Tyler watched them. "Doctor," he said, "why are you cutting here? Why are you cutting there? Why do you hold the knife that way?" And they told him. At lunch, Tyler went to the library and withdrew mysteries and anatomy books. At night, he and Rose lay in their big wooden bed and he read to her. Rose was blind. Tyler put his arm around her small body and whispered, "Chief, listen to this."

Soon the surgeons were calling to say, "Allen, you know how to do this. Can you get two knees ready for me?"

"No problem," Tyler said proudly. "I'll prepare those for you right away, Doctor." Though he was tentative at first, Tyler gained confidence as he perfected his skills with the knife. After a few years, he was able to detach a shoulder with a few clean cuts. When he sawed off a knee, he learned to place his saw exactly twelve inches above the kneecap. He could cut up an entire body in less than half an hour.

"Allen loved doing what he did," Rose said. "A lot of years, he never took sick days or a vacation. I used to tell him, those white doctors and everyone else takes time off—why can't you?" But her husband was adamant.

Tyler's hard work paid off. In 1975, UTMB promoted him to supervisor of Anatomical Services. Dressed in slacks and an Oxford shirt, a silk ascot at his neck and a derby tipped stylishly on his head, Tyler strolled each day in and out of the Romanesque redbrick building on the UTMB campus. In the lobby, he ambled past the stone sculptures of famous doctors on display—Hippocrates, Louis Pasteur, Joseph Lister, and others. He liked to greet the students as he passed: "Good morning, ladies. Good morning, sir." People who didn't know Tyler often mistook him for a doctor. Tyler smiled but didn't correct them.

A good diener is hard to find, and UTMB was happy to have Tyler. He was gentle with grief-stricken family members who called, attentive to the museum of specimens preserved in formaldehyde, careful to lay out the bodies each day and to keep the cadaver tanks in the basement clean.

By 1997, Allen Tyler was running the willed-body program. Over the years, it had undergone significant changes. When Tyler started in the lab, the department didn't even have a freezer. They didn't need one, since the school never provided fresh cadavers or body parts to outside researchers or vendors. All of the bodies stayed right there in the lab so that the students and doctors could use them.

But the demand for corpses and body parts had grown.

By the 1990s, the university was providing dozens of specimens every year to outside vendors. Nearly a dozen meat freezers filled with parts now lined the lab. The school had become a well-known source of corpses, and people were calling for specimens all the time.

Tyler had a speech that he gave to buyers. He informed them that it was against the law to buy and sell bodies. The school charged a fee for each part, but it was just to recover its costs. A buyer who wanted parts would have to write to the state anatomy board for permission. Dr. Andrew Payer was the board's secretary treasurer as well as Tyler's boss. The board was responsible for registering every cadaver donated to the Texas university system. Payer collected the fees and reviewed every request. Tyler could only "sell" body parts with the board's approval.

Tyler's stern stance didn't faze Augie Perna. In 1997, Perna called looking for some torsos. Records show that he applied for and received permission from the board. Then Tyler sent him the torsos he needed.

But by 1998, things had started to go wrong. The man who never missed work, who never called in sick, who never took a vacation, was now working as Perna's consultant, taking time off and flying around the country to attend surgical conferences.

A taxi now arrived regularly at Tyler's home. While it idled at the curb, Tyler kissed Rose and said, "I'm going to work with the doctors." Rose was thrilled with Tyler's new duties. "He said the doctors were very friendly," she recalled.

Knowing that his wife would never see the places he visited, Tyler regaled her with funny stories when he returned. He described the people in New York—how silly they looked wrapped up like mummies in hats and scarves when it was seven below. He described the sumptuous dinners he shared with the doctors, how they ate sushi in Savannah and oysters at the famous Union Oyster House in Boston and crabs in San Francisco. Tyler brought her souvenirs such as T-shirts and delicate porcelain angels for her curio collection.

In 2000, Tyler began flying out to California to cut up corpses for Michael Brown. His best friend, Kenneth Carter, assumed he'd been promoted. "I was so happy for him," he said. Tyler sent Carter postcards highlighting the sunny climes of the West Coast. "It was cold here, but wherever he was the weather was nice."

Tyler's daughter, Nina, had noticed subtle changes in her father. He had started wearing blue jeans and cowboy boots. "Mama," she said, "Daddy's style is changing."

"Hmm," Rose teased her husband. "Who are you taking out?"

But her husband just smiled and teased her back.

No one but Tyler knew that when an especially choice body was donated to UTMB, he was reporting it as "damaged" in the school database, cutting it up, entering each part into his own database, and selling the parts off to Augie Perna's companies and others. No one knew that he replaced UTMB's invoices with his own so that vendors could pay him directly. No one knew that when he attended

Perna's conferences as a consultant, he was also supplying the bodies and getting paid for them under the guise of an honorarium.

Tyler shipped the torsos straight to the hotels so they'd be waiting for him at the front desk. Late at night, he lugged the coolers up to his room to prepare them for the next day.

Over a period of three years, Tyler sold more than a thousand body parts belonging to the university—knees, shoulders, torsos, and elbows—and earned upward of $200,000, according to the FBI. Between November 1999 and August 2001, from fingernails and toenails alone he made at least $18,210. When he started to receive checks at home, Tyler installed a new mailbox with a lock.

Like Michael Brown, Tyler was becoming the man he'd always wanted to be: admired by doctors and revered by his friends and his wife. As the money came in, Tyler told Rose that they could finally remodel the kitchen. He moved his wife into a nearby apartment so that she'd be comfortable during the construction. Then he had the roof on their bungalow replaced and the siding redone. He had a brand-new dishwasher installed in the kitchen, then new cabinets, a stainless-steel refrigerator, and a new stove. To reward himself, he bought a $40,000 Lexus SUV and a Rolex watch.

But Allen Tyler was getting careless. He was cataloguing bodies with numbers that hadn't even been assigned yet by the anatomy board. He had stopped sending blood samples from cadavers to the lab and was commingling ashes in a fifty-gallon drum. When it was time to return ashes to a family, he scooped out a bagful and shipped them off. Tyler never suspected he'd be caught.

Then, in December 2001, just as Tyler was settling into his new life, he got a visit from Detective Rene Rodriguez. Rodriguez told Tyler that he was investigating Michael Brown's crematorium in southern California, and he asked Tyler if he'd meet him and another detective at the Hilton Resort, a modern hotel overlooking the gray waters of the Gulf of Mexico in Galveston. That day, according to his notes, Rodriguez asked Tyler about his responsibilities at the university. Tyler replied that he taught medical students basic anatomy. When Rodriguez asked him how, with only a high school diploma and no documents certifying him as an anatomist, he had learned the skill of dissection. Tyler said he gained the experience "on the job."

Tyler admitted dismembering corpses for Brown, but he said he didn't know anything about Brown's body-parts company or how Brown had decided what bodies should be disarticulated. After two hours, the interview ended and Detective Rodriguez flew back to California.

Tyler assumed he had escaped detection. But in March 2002, according to FBI documents, the Riverside County District Attorney's Office contacted UTMB to verify Tyler's claims about his employment. The phone call spurred the university to review Tyler's travel records, which, in turn, revealed a series of questionable invoices concerning "honoraria" that Tyler had sent Perna. Concerned, the medical school's comptrollers passed the invoices on to UTMB police, who alerted the FBI.

One look at the documents and FBI Agent Jim Walsh knew this was a case of fraud. He requested that the university conduct an internal audit of the program. By April 2002, the audit was complete. Just as Walsh had suspected, it revealed fraudulent billing. Walsh wanted to send in an undercover agent to buy parts from Tyler. But before he could set up the sting, the university's legal department sent Tyler a letter telling him he'd been suspended pending an investigation.

Walsh knew that as soon as Tyler read the letter, the sting would be off. Hoping to intercept the letter from the mailman, he raced to Tyler's home with two UTMB police officers. The storm shutters on the bungalow were closed. Walsh parked around the corner and waited. By nightfall, neither the mailman nor Tyler had showed. Walsh went home and returned early the next morning. Suddenly, from his car, he saw the shutters move. Tyler had been watching him the whole time.

"The jig is up," Walsh said. "He knows we're outside, and we need to go talk to him."

"Allen, I know you're in there," he said, sidling up to the door. "I know you can hear me. I want to talk to you." The storm shutters opened a crack on the back door. "I know you can see me," Walsh said, holding up his ID. "I'd like to talk to you."

"Do you have a warrant? Are you here to arrest me?" Tyler stammered.

"I don't have a warrant, and I'm not here to arrest you."

"Well, go ahead. What do you want to talk about?"

"I've talked to some people over at UTMB and I've heard some things that they have to say, and I'd like to talk to you about it," Walsh said gently. "I'm trying to find out what's going on here."

Tyler unlocked the door. "Who's that with you?" he asked.

"He's with the university police department," Walsh said, gesturing to the man with him. "Can we come in?"

"Yeah, come on in."

The house was dark and damp. The shutters were closed, and the lights were off. Tyler's medications for the prostate cancer he'd been battling lay about the messy living room. In the kitchen, plastic jars of spices covered the counters. Clothes wrapped in plastic were draped over the furniture. The dining room set had been pushed into the center of the room. Around it were books and papers. Tyler had cleared a pathway through the clutter to get to and from the windows. The letter from the university lay open on the dining room table.

There was nowhere to sit, so Agent Walsh grabbed a folding chair. Tyler faced him, slumped over in a dining room chair.

"I'm trying to find out what's going on here," Walsh said. "Personally, I don't think I need to be involved in this, and I want to talk to you about it and we can clear the air and I can move on to doing other things that I need to be doing. So if you can just tell me what it is that you do there at the university . . ."

Tyler talked for an hour and a half. The more he talked,

the more confident he was that he could bluff his way out of trouble. He didn't know that Walsh had already seen the invoices or that the audit had revealed his fraud. Soon, he was strutting around the house, gesturing to Walsh and describing how carefully he ran the program. He insisted there were never any deviations from the proper procedures for the cadavers.

"Let's take a break," Walsh said, getting up. After five minutes, he sat down again. "Okay, Allen, is there anything else that you can think of that you left out?"

Tyler shook his head.

Then Walsh took out the invoices.

The instant Tyler saw them, he shrunk back in his chair and stared at the carpet.

"Can you see these?" Walsh asked, thrusting the invoices in Tyler's face.

"Yeah, I see 'em. I see 'em." Tyler was now squirming in his chair.

"Get a good look. Do you recognize these? That's your name on there." Walsh held the papers out, forcing Tyler to take them in his hands.

"I don't have anything to say about them," Tyler said. But his shaking hands betrayed him.

Walsh assured him he knew everything, how Tyler had stolen bodies and sold them and that the honoraria were really sales.

Tyler began to sob. Tears poured down his face.

Walsh produced an invoice for $4,800 for a one-day

conference in Pennsylvania hosted by Perna's company, Surgical Body Forms. The description of the service listed eight "honoraria."

"How can you get honoraria on your time off for eight days when the course was only a day and you've only taken one day off from work?" Walsh barked. "See where the problem is here?"

Tyler nodded.

But Walsh wasn't after just Tyler. He was also after the middlemen. In the hopes of going ahead with the sting, Walsh told Tyler he wanted to bring him into the fold. "Here's how it would work," he said. "You'd operate in the business with our okay. You'd be working for us now. We need to know who your contacts are and who you're shipping all this stuff to. It's to your benefit. Unless you come out and help us, you're going to take the hit for everything."

Tyler cried harder. He told Walsh he couldn't do it. He'd spent all night burning up the phones. Everyone in the body-parts business knew he was as good as fired and that the auditors were all over his office. Tyler told Walsh that he was afraid he'd end up like the bodies he'd been selling.

Walsh left his card. "If you ever change your mind," he said, "just call me."

Tyler never called. By November 2002, Walsh had turned over the case to the U.S. Attorney's office for prosecution. But Allen Tyler was never charged with a crime. In 2003, he was called to testify, but was too ill to appear.

Then, in January 2004, he succumbed to cancer. With their main witness deceased, the U.S. Attorney's Office decided not to press its case.

The University of Pennsylvania, the University of Michigan, and the University of Texas Medical Branch are in no way alone in their involvement with the cadaver trade. According to internal documents and police investigations, dieners at many prestigious universities have supplied the underground body business. Dieners at the University of California–Irvine, Western University of Health Sciences in Pomona, California, and the University of California–Los Angeles have all been implicated in the underground cadaver trade.

Between 1998 and 2005, criminal investigations have been launched into four different medical schools. But amazingly, as of this writing, apart from the University of Pennsylvania dieners, only one medical school employee— at Western University of Health Sciences—has been indicted or served jail time.

UCLA was the first of these medical schools to have its scandal on the front page of the *New York Times*. In 2004, the diener at UCLA, Henry Reid, was arrested for allegedly selling body parts to a broker and pocketing the profits. Once again, the administrators appeared stunned by the news. "The allegations of criminal activity involving the Willed-Body Program are extremely troubling," UCLA chancellor Albert Carnasale said. "Please know that we are shocked and angered by the despicable behavior of those involved."

It was the second time that the school's willed-body program had come under scrutiny. In 1996, donor families had filed a class-action suit against UCLA for cremating the bodies of their loved ones in piles with medical waste and sending the ashes to a landfill, after promising to bury them or scatter them in a rose garden.

After the '96 scandal, UCLA administrators hired Henry Reid to clean up the program. Had they looked more closely, they would have found plenty of signs that he wasn't the right man for the job. Reid went on to lie under oath in a 2002 deposition relating to a donor family's lawsuit against the school. He claimed to have a master's degree from Cal State Fullerton. He also claimed to have graduated *summa cum laude* from Cypress College. In fact, he did not have a master's, and Cypress College does not award degrees *summa cum laude*. What he did have was financial trouble. Two years after he went to work for UCLA, he filed for bankruptcy. He owed creditors more than $100,000.

Not long after that, Reid went into business with a local broker named Ernest V. Nelson. Over the next four years, Reid allegedly sold hundreds of cadavers to Nelson, who cut them up into parts and then resold them out of his garage to companies like Mitek, a Johnson & Johnson company, which used them to develop orthopedic surgical devices. Records provided to the *Los Angeles Times* by Nelson's law firm showed that Nelson paid Reid three quarters of a million dollars for the body parts, which Reid then allegedly pocketed.

In March 2004, Reid and Nelson were arrested by UCLA police for grand theft and receiving stolen property. They are now free on bail and have still not been charged. As of this writing, families of donors to the school are suing UCLA. In an attempt to have the case dismissed, UCLA lawyers have argued that the school was free to do as it wished with its donated bodies, including selling them to companies, as long as the bodies were used for education and research. The judge in the case has sided with the families, and the lawsuits are proceeding.

In the case of the University of Texas Medical Branch, the university has argued that it has sovereign immunity, a constitutional right derived from the Eleventh Amendment. Sovereign immunity protects public universities from being sued. The courts upheld UTMB's immunity. None of the half-dozen lawsuits filed by the victims' families have moved forward. Until this book, the information obtained by the FBI was never reported.

The universities' real strategy seems to have been to keep the American public in the dark and to whitewash any involvement that they might have with body brokers. Some schools have a lot to hide, and their dieners aren't the only ones to blame. Cadaver money tempts even the illustrious chairmen of the anatomy departments.

It's common for medical schools with a surplus of donated bodies to share them with other schools. While the supplying schools don't always tell donors about this possibility, most medical schools try to carry out the exchange as respectfully as possible. Ideally, a school in need contacts a school with a surplus and together they negotiate the exchange. The supplying school is given approval over how the bodies are used, when and by whom they are transported and later cremated. Together, the schools establish a fair price to reimburse the supplying school for the costs of preparing and storing the bodies. Usually, these fees are nominal.

But in some cases, schools with a surplus of corpses hire middlemen to broker the bodies for them. Brokers are willing to buy bodies in bulk. They pick the bodies up, carry them away, find customers for them—sometimes recycling a single body for use by multiple customers—and dispose of the remains.

Donors and their families do not expect money to be made from their donations. But when a school sells bodies to a broker, there's no way to ensure this expectation is met. By nature, brokers are businessmen and thus, once they've paid for a corpse, they feel entitled to make a profit. When a school sells a body to a broker, the school has no control over how the body will be used, or when and by whom, and how much the buyers will be charged.

Still, using brokers is a great way for a school to generate income. Some medical schools regularly engage in business with body brokers. The University of Texas Southwestern, the University of Kansas School of Medicine, Washington University School of Medicine, Tulane School of Medicine, and Louisiana State University Health Sciences Center in Shreveport have all worked with body brokers.

One broker who has done a brisk business with medical schools is John Vincent Scalia, who owns the John Vincent Scalia Home for Funerals on Staten Island. Until April 2004, he also owned an outfit called National Anatomical Service. Since the 1970s, Scalia has held a highly profitable monopoly on surplus university cadavers. In addition to brokering deals between schools, Scalia has sold body parts to doctors, to a crematorium in Chicago, and to other brokers.

Scalia is discreet about the service he provides and about his university clients. In a 2002 interview, he claimed to be out of the cadaver trade entirely. Meanwhile, that same year, he sold the military nine bodies for $37,485.

Steve Rountree was his Army contact. Rountree had been hired to find dead bodies for Colonel Robert Harris, a renowned Army surgeon who needed the bodies to test ballistic armor for humanitarian deminers who work detonating mines all over the world. The bodies had to be fresh, male, and under seventy-two years old.

Such bodies are hard to come by.

Luckily, John Vincent Scalia was more than happy to help out. As is customary, Scalia disclosed little to Rountree about his operation. Rountree didn't even know that Scalia owned a funeral home. He did know that the bodies Scalia sold him came from Louisiana State University and Tulane School of Medicine.

On the surface, this was a perfectly reasonable scenario: two medical schools collaborating with the Army to save the lives of deminers. If anyone should provide cadavers to the Army, a medical school is a logical choice. But the Army still needs consent from the donors and their families. If the deal is done right, the school and the Army work together, finding a suitable mode of transportation and agreeing on a reasonable fee to get the bodies to and from Louisiana. The Army might reimburse the school for the cost of storing the bodies and preparing them for the journey.

But that was not the case here. The Army had signed a contract with a body broker. LSU and Tulane were peripheral.

Founded in 1834 as the Medical College of Louisiana, Tulane is the second-oldest medical school in the Deep South and the first school of its kind in Louisiana. A group of young, idealistic doctors founded the school after arriving in New Orleans and finding the city plagued by cholera and overrun with poorly trained physicians. Pooling their resources, Dr. Thomas Hunt, Dr. John Hoffman Harrison, Dr. Charles Luzenberg, and Dr. Warren Stone established the school hoping to "advance the cause of science," according to their announcement in the local newspaper.

Anatomy was the centerpiece of the new school's curriculum. "How can he repair the derangements of structures, who does not know what structure is?" Dr. Hunt asked in a speech to the first freshman class. The school offered dissection courses regularly. Unlike anatomy professors in some parts of the country, the professors at Tulane had no trouble obtaining corpses. There were plenty of bodies to be had from the charity hospital.

The Medical College of Louisiana went on to become one of the finest medical schools in the country. It has produced some of the great medical innovators of our time, like Michael E. DeBakey, who pioneered the artificial heart. Years of success have inspired loyalty and enthusiasm among neighbors and alumni, many of whom have donated their bodies to the school's very successful willed-body program. While some schools suffer from perennial cadaver shortages, Tulane gets many more bodies than it needs.

Tulane University Medical School has supplied National Anatomical Service with corpses for more than a decade. Tulane charged Scalia $960 for each corpse. Scalia then resold the bodies at his own rate. Those he sold to the Army he marked up by more than 400 percent.

When I reached him by phone in 2002, Dr. Gerald Kirby, who was then chairman of the Anatomy Department, denied knowing anything about National Anatomical Service. "I don't know what National Anatomical Service does," he said. But later, he acknowledged using them. "NAS works as a broker, which is very useful for us. One-third of the bodies we receive are brokered by National Anatomical Service," he said. Then he paused. "Brokered sounds bad, doesn't it? I don't know what the right word is."

Many people wouldn't sell any gift they were given—not even a dress or a pair of shoes. But some universities think nothing of selling bodies. People who donate their bodies to a school like Tulane expect their bodies to be helping first-

year medical students at Tulane. Donors often have an emo-
tional attachment to a particular school and would never
have willingly donated their body to another school. The
schools know this well, which is why they are so loath to
admit that they sell bodies to outsiders.

Kirby wouldn't reveal how many bodies the school
receives every year. "If that's something that becomes public, people might say, 'You're getting too many, we're not
going to donate,'" he said. But according to a BBC report,
Tulane receives about 150 bodies every year. If one-third of
them are brokered every year, as Kirby claims, then as many
as 500 Tulane donors may have entered the underground
cadaver trade over the last ten years.

When word of Tulane's dealings with the Army hit the
news, the public reacted with outrage, just as Kirby had
feared. "You know what's the worst of it for me?" one
woman told a reporter at the *Times-Picayune*. "My father's
got this image of the woman he loved being blown up by
the Army." Another woman said, "That made me ill, the
idea of the fees and the money collected. . . . It smacked of
the 1800s and grave robbing."

Rather than address the families' concerns, Scalia feigned
ignorance. In one interview with the *New York Post*, he
denied ever selling bodies to the Army, claiming instead that
he had deposited the bodies at a Virginia medical school,
which then passed them on to the Army without his knowledge. He claimed he did business only with universities.

Tulane officials also denied knowing that the bodies
were going to the Army. But Dr. Kirby had approved this

very transfer himself. "I got a call from Colonel Baker in the summer," Kirby said. "He asked me if I thought it was appropriate to use the cadaver for that purpose. My first reaction was 'No, this is medical stuff,' and then I said, 'Hey, this is right on! This is prophylactic medicine.'"

Kirby said that Colonel Baker had asked him if he thought they should call the families and get their permission before blowing up their loved ones.

Kirby said he had thought about it and had replied, "Nah, nah. Ugly."

"It's much better if there isn't any possibility of irrational speculation," he later explained.

Land mine experiments are just one example of what became of some Tulane donors. In 2003, June Reynolds donated her husband, Charley, to Tulane. A brilliant, eccentric engineer, Charley had always wanted to donate his body to science. Tulane was a natural choice. As a college senior, Charley was invited to apply to the medical school because of his exceptional grades. He became an engineer instead. But now, he would finally get to go. At seventy-nine, he was an excellent specimen: six feet two, lean and muscular, like a teenage athlete.

The donation went smoothly. Charley died on a Sunday. On Wednesday, someone from the school came to pick him up at the funeral home. When June Reynolds called the school later that day, Tulane's diener, Kenneth Webb, told her that her husband's body had been embalmed and was all set to be used in an anatomy course.

One year later, Reynolds read an article about Tulane

and the Army in the *Times-Picayune* and grew concerned. After several frustrating phone calls back and forth to Tulane during which, she said, she got the impression that "people either didn't know where Charley was or they didn't want to tell me," she finally learned that her husband's body had never been embalmed. In fact, the school had frozen him and sold him to National Anatomical Service. Two and a half months after Charley died, National Anatomical picked him up, drove him to Detroit, and dumped him at Arthur Rathburn's headquarters. Rathburn had slated Charley for a hip-replacement course at a resort in Vail, Colorado.

The family was devastated, but Charley's daughter also recalled a sweet irony. Her father had always loved to travel. He'd lived all over the world, in some of the most primitive places, and he had never needed much to feel at home: just a cot, a car, and an airplane to get around. "He would try to come home to live," she said, "but he was too restless, so he would be off again as soon as possible. The fact that we all thought he was over at Tulane quietly being a contribution, and then found out that he had been at least two or three other places—it was just the sort of thing that would happen with Dad."

Charley would have probably enjoyed a trip to Vail, but his family was desperate to get his body back. "Something limbic, something primordial comes up," his daughter Jane said. "We had to keep at it until we got him home." Fortunately, they got to Charley in time. He was waiting peacefully in cold storage in Detroit.

June Reynolds was grateful to have her husband back. But she's still suspicious of the whole process. "Every time we got some information, it was erroneous."

Tulane got most of the attention, but Louisiana State University was also selling bodies to Scalia. In 2002, Scalia, who pays LSU $600 for each cadaver, sold five LSU bodies to the Army for more than $20,000. LSU has been making quite a bit of money from donated cadavers—$246,200, to be exact, between 1998 and 2004—and that is just from transfers to National Anatomical Service. Most of the money appears to have gone to the department of Cellular Biology and Anatomy. The chairman of the department, Dr. Leonard Seelig, told me that the cadaver fees simply cover their costs. But one NAS check was made out to the mysteriously named "Anatomy Club Fund." No such club exists at LSU. Seelig offered two different explanations for how he used the money. First, he claimed the money went to pay the living expenses of international students. Later, he said he used it to pay students to clean out the cadaver tanks, though this is usually the diener's job.

Seelig, who says he has obtained all of the necessary clearance to send bodies out of state, doesn't see any problem with hiring a broker to distribute surplus cadavers. "We have had problems throughout the years with many people who donate their bodies, but I've never had any problem with John Scalia."

This is not surprising, since Seelig told me that he doesn't concern himself with the particulars. He sells bodies and gets back ashes. He never investigates where the bodies end up, nor does he know where Scalia does the cremations. "John Scalia takes care of that, and I just take his word for it. He has assured me that they go to other medical centers."

LSU has, in essence, become a corpse wholesaler, but there is some confusion about whether or not this is an acceptable practice. When I called LSU's Director of Accounting Services, Janie Binderim, she appeared to be unaware of the cadaver sales. She says it would be illegal for the school to sell bodies. "As a nonprofit institution, we cannot generate revenue." As an example, she offered the case of one of the school's research departments, which proposed leasing some of its equipment to an outside company. "We had to tell them that they can't do that. We're a charity institution," she said. "We encourage people to donate their bodies, but we don't go out to sell those bodies to earn additional income." For his part, John Scalia strongly objects to being called a broker and says he simply gets paid for transporting cadavers.

Binderim added that even if the Anatomy Department was simply transferring the bodies elsewhere and being reimbursed for its costs, it would still be a violation of the school's accounting policy. "It really doesn't have to do with whether you make a profit. If we obtain revenue that is not part of our original mission, which, as a charity hospital, is to take care of indigent patients, then we are subject to an unrelated business tax."

Not only do the cadaver sales appear to violate the mission of Louisiana State University, but they also violate Louisiana state law, which prohibits the transfer of any body out of state unless the body is being used for education by a doctor licensed in Louisiana or by an employee of a Louisiana medical school. The penalty is a $200 fine or imprisonment for not more than one year. But the Louisiana attorney general has no plans to investigate.

Tulane claims to have cut all ties with Scalia, but LSU continues to do business with his company, despite outcries from the public. Scalia, meanwhile, has dissolved National Anatomical Service and surrendered the license granted to him by the New York State Department of Health. Technically, National Anatomical Service no longer exists, but John Vincent Scalia is still very much in business. As of this writing, he has continued to buy corpses from the University of Kansas. But without a license or a legitimate registered company, he's operating more covertly than ever.

———

In June 2004, the American Association of Clinical Anatomists met on the picturesque campus of Saint Mary's College in Moraga, California. Hundreds of anatomists had come from all over the world. They were a serious, thoughtful bunch—predominantly men dressed in button-downs and khakis.

The scandals at UCLA and Tulane had just broken, and the mood at the conference was tense. On the first day, two anatomists could be seen sitting outside the auditorium on a stone bench in the shade. They sat with their hands clasped, their anxious gazes fixed on the sunburnt hilltops in the distance.

It had been fourteen years since the members of the

AACA met in Saskatchewan to discuss body brokers. Since then, it seemed that more and more willed-body programs were being exploited by companies, greedy dieners, and even medical schools themselves. In response to the most recent scandals, the AACA had dedicated an entire morning session to the issue of the underground traffic. They invited Louis Marlin, the lawyer representing UCLA in the body-brokering case, an auditor from UC Irvine Medical School, which had recently revamped its donor program after a body-theft scandal in 1999, and a representative from the California Department of Health.

In a separate meeting, members of the original 1990 group drafted specific recommendations for donor programs, including a recommendation that the willed-body programs be properly supervised by faculty and that there be an approval process for outsiders requesting specimens. It was clear that this group was anxious to do the right thing, to educate its members, and to ensure that donor programs around the country honored the wishes of the people who had so generously given their bodies.

But there was also a sense of despair and frustration among the AACA members. As one man pointed out, the organization has no authority to enforce its recommendations. The anatomists can't police each other, let alone the surgical equipment companies that work with brokers. Anatomists have become the gatekeepers to a lucrative commodity. Yet so long as there was little state regulation, no federal oversight, and a market for body parts, the incidents of profiteering and theft would continue to plague their schools.

"People who believe that all it's going to take is each individual school creating policies and hiring people with integrity are kidding themselves," said one California anatomist. "These third-party people are not operating under the same sort of understanding we are about educating people. They're in business."

For all of the efforts of organizations like the AACA to wrestle with the underground trade in corpses, the surgical-equipment companies have been largely silent. In the case of UCLA, Johnson & Johnson admitted that one of its subsidiaries, DePuy Mitek, bought body parts from broker Ernest Nelson between 1996 and 1999. But the company claims that it "did not knowingly receive samples that may have been obtained in an inappropriate way."

"We take the matter of using human tissue samples for medical research and education very seriously," Sarah Colamarino, a spokesperson, wrote in an e-mail. "DePuy Mitek follows all applicable regulatory requirements and guidelines in using anatomical specimens for medical research and education."

But how could they not have known? Nelson claimed to represent the University of California system of medical schools, but he was never in the school's employ and worked out of his home. The serology reports detailing blood test results from the body parts that he supplied to clients resembled something a child might create from a Microsoft Word template, complete with a microscope logo, as if microscopes were used to test for HIV and hepatitis C. Viruses are simply too small to be detected under a regular microscope. In fact, labs use special kits, not microscopes, to test for the antibodies that the body produces as a result of infection with viruses like HIV. Nowhere on the reports was the name of the lab where the so-called testing was done. There was no federal lab ID number or medical director listed as the law requires. Even to a layperson, the paperwork Nelson supplied would have been suspect.

But Nelson's clients apparently never raised alarm bells. Nor did Allen Tyler's clients. After using Nelson, Mitek went on to buy shoulders and knees from Michael Brown's company. They did what they have always done. They bought body parts wherever they could get them. When one broker folded up shop, they found another willing broker. And the business carried on.

chapter 7

The Bone Machine

For the most part, all bodies undisturbed after death decay in the same way. The rate of decay can vary dramatically according to variables in temperature, humidity, place, and cause of death. But the decay is relentless. As soon as the heart stops pumping, blood settles in the lowermost part of the corpse. The body cools. The muscles relax and then stiffen—first the eyes, then the neck, then the jaw go into rigor mortis. The rest of the body follows part by part.

By the third day, a green tinge has spread across the torso and down the thighs. Bacteria now devour the flesh. Their foul gas inflates the body, drives the bowel from the rectum, and forces bloody liquid from the nose and mouth. The skin blisters, loosens, and peels.

By the third week, the heart, liver, and kidney begin to rupture and liquefy. Soon, there is nothing left but bones.

Early one morning in September 2001, a young man in Utah shot himself. His father found him, lying in his room, a .22-caliber handgun by his side. The young man had been out late the night before. His father had heard him stumble in at around 1:30 in the morning. But no one heard the shot. The medical examiner ruled his death a suicide.

By the time his father found him, the young man had been dead for almost nineteen hours. The process of decay had begun. While the young man lay dead in his bedroom, *Clostridium sordelli* bacteria probably broke from his bowel through his intestinal wall and began circulating through his body.

At the medical examiner's office, an official approached the young man's parents about donating their son's tissue for transplant. The parents agreed and signed the paperwork. Their son, now officially Donor 58600, was transferred to the local tissue bank.

Once Bart Wheatley of Intermountain Donor Services got the body, he set about locating a buyer. Donor 58600 was well past the twelve-hour time limit that a donor body can remain without refrigeration if its tissue is meant to be transplanted. Wheatley knew right off the bat that several regular customers would turn him down, including the processor that had the right of first refusal on all of Intermountain's musculoskeletal tissue. It wasn't even worth making the call.

But for every corpse—no matter how far gone—there is

a willing buyer. Wheatley called CryoLife, a tissue processor in Georgia that paid handsomely. He got a guy on the phone named Matt and gave him all the details. Matt told him to send the tissue of Donor 58600 along. By nightfall, it was packed on ice and on a plane to Atlanta. Cryolife paid $10,500 for the tissue.

A couple of months later, a section of Donor 58600's knee would wind up in St. Cloud, Minnesota.

On the seventh of November 2001, a twenty-three-year-old man named Brian Lykins was admitted to St. Cloud Hospital in Minnesota for what was to be routine knee surgery. Lykins was young, full of hope for the future, a creative man who taught himself to play the piano by listening to tapes of classical music. Lykins had recently moved home to Minnesota to be closer to his family and was taking classes in electrical engineering at a local college.

Though he was in perfect health, an operation to remove a bone chip in his knee had left Lykins with a quarter-sized divot in his knee. To prevent arthritis in the future and return his knee to its normal state, his surgeon, Dr. Mulawka, suggested that he have another procedure to fill in the gap. Dr. Mulawka explained that he would use a piece of bone donated from a cadaver to repair the hole. He assured Brian and his parents that there was nothing to worry about. It was common to use donated tissue in healthy patients. The tissue, he said, had been tested and was free of disease.

Because Brian was young and healthy, complications from the procedure were highly unlikely. Dr. Mulawka warned that, at worst, Brian might become slightly sick from the postoperative medications and possibly experience more pain than he had after his first surgery—such reactions were common, but they usually resolved quickly and were followed by a speedy recovery.

The operation proceeded without incident. No one was surprised when Brian went into recovery in a lot of pain. That was natural after any surgery. But Brian also had a headache and an upset stomach, and he complained to the nurses that he felt hot. When they took his temperature, however, it was normal and his other vital signs looked good. Still, as a precaution, Dr. Mulawka suggested that Brian stay in the hospital overnight. By the time his parents were ready to leave the hospital that evening, Brian was resting comfortably in his room, and the doctor assured everyone that he would be discharged the next day.

That night, Brian threw up and the pain in his knee got worse. The hospital staff suspected he was having a reaction to the medication, which was being administered through a pain pack inserted in his knee, and the pack was subsequently removed. The next day, Brian was discharged, and by the time he got home, he was feeling much better. His knee was still a little bit sore and he said he felt a little warm, but otherwise, he was starting to feel like himself again. It seemed as if Brian was on the road to recovery.

Two days later, however, Brian's condition changed. He began throwing up violently, almost passing out twice on his way to the sink. He complained to his mother that he had that hot feeling again, but when she touched his face, it was perfectly cool. Alarmed, Mrs. Lykins called the hospital and left a message for the doctor. A few minutes later, someone from the hospital called back and told her to change the dosage on one of Brian's medications. But Brian was feeling unsettlingly sick, so he returned to the hospital to be examined.

Mrs. Lykins drove Brian to St. Cloud, where he was examined in the emergency room by a nurse and a doctor, both of whom attributed his symptoms to dehydration. They put him on an IV and gave him something to settle his stomach. Still, Brian, whose face had turned a strange shade of gray, wasn't getting better. He lay in bed, sweating profusely, stripping off his shirt and his blankets. The pain in his knee was unbearable. Twice he doubled over and vomited green liquid.

Again, the nurse couldn't find the source of the problem. His knee was not swollen or red. He had no fever. His blood pressure and his heart rate were normal. The doctor ordered a chest X-ray and had blood drawn from Brian. No one knew what to make of his symptoms.

Around midnight, Mrs. Lykins went out to get some rest in the ER waiting room. Shortly after, a nurse tapped her on the shoulder. Brian's blood pressure had plummeted unexpectedly. When Mrs. Lykins came into her son's room, she found a group of doctors working anxiously around him. One of them asked Mrs. Lykins if there was anyone she wanted to contact. Terrified, she called her husband. In the meantime, Brian was transferred to intensive care. His heart was racing and his body was struggling to get enough oxygen. At one point, he sat up in bed and groaned. Then he fell into a coma. By the time his father arrived, Brian's organs were failing, one by one. His heart was the last to go. At 6:21 A.M., Brian Lykins died—and no one at the hospital could explain why.

That was before anyone knew about Donor 58600.

It was several days before the donated cartilage was pinpointed as the cause of Lykins's death. It was weeks before the journey of Donor 58600 was discovered, weeks before health officials located all of its many pieces, and months before a national investigation by the Centers for Disease Control revealed twenty-five more cases of serious infections in patients who had had similar operations. One of them, a seventeen-year-old boy in Illinois, also received tissue from Donor 58600. The infection nearly destroyed his knee joint.

It's likely that none of this would have been discovered if, one day after Lykins died, another knee surgery patient at St. Cloud Hospital hadn't also died after going under the knife. A few days later, a third person at a different Minnesota hospital died after knee surgery. These two cases didn't involve transplant tissue and later turned out to be unrelated to Lykins's death. But they caused health department officials to take the rare step of declaring a moratorium on elective knee surgery in the state of Minnesota and to launch a major investigation with the CDC.

Officials hunted everywhere for clues. Fearing the deaths might have been caused by a hospital-acquired infection, they sent out packages of surgical drapes and samples of the iodine solution used to clean Brian's skin before surgery. They toured the surgical suites, searching for signs of recent construction or problems with ventilation. They scoured surgery records looking for similar incidents—anything that might shed light on what had happened.

No one was prepared for Lykins's blood results. In the lab, his blood had grown *Clostridium sordelli,* which is often found in soil and farm animals. It's rarely found in humans. Health officials were stumped. "All of us were running to the books," said Dr. Mei Castor, an epidemiologist at the Minnesota Department of Heath. "It is a very rare thing to find."

For weeks, the press ran front-page stories about the case. Citizens were outraged. Patients were worried, and the phones were ringing off the hook at the Centers for Disease Control. Hundreds of people called demanding answers about tissue banking.

In Wisconsin, Bonny Gonyer read about Lykins in her local paper. She had received a tissue transplant in her knee a few months before Brian Lykins had. She, too, had developed a mysterious infection and could barely walk. Luckily, Gonyer's doctors cultured her blood in time and discovered *Clostridium.* They told her they didn't know what had caused the infection, but they gave her intravenous antibiotics. Slowly, Gonyer got better.

Then, a few months before Lykins died, Gonyer

relapsed. *Clostridium,* which exists as tiny egglike spores, can live dormant in the body and suddenly awaken. This time, doctors blamed the metal screws they'd used. They performed an emergency operation and replaced the screws. But they left the cadaver tissue inside.

Gonyer was no longer able to kneel or crawl. She needed someone with her at all times, in case she fell. She couldn't run around or play with her teenage sons. The household tasks she had once done with ease were now exhausting.

Still, no one—not even Gonyer—suspected the cadaver tissue in her knee. Then Gonyer read the article about Lykins in the paper. When she confronted her surgeon, she learned that her tissue had also come from CryoLife. But the hospital, never suspecting the tissue, hadn't reported her infection to the company. If they had, it might have saved Brian Lykins's life.

———

The practice of transplanting human tissue began in the late 1940s as an experiment. Several surgeons had reported success transplanting frozen bone. In 1949, George Hyatt, an innovative orthopedic surgeon at the Naval Medical Center in Maryland, convinced the chairman of the orthopedic department at the Naval Hospital to buy a small freezer and let Hyatt and several colleagues use frozen bone transplants. Hyatt began storing bones removed from patients during surgery, which he and his colleagues used to repair fractures in other patients.

The experiment was a success. Soon Hyatt and his colleagues needed a bigger freezer. They also needed a more consistent supply of bone tissue, so they turned to cadavers. Because the surgeons were implanting the tissue, the bodies had to be fresh and free of disease. The bodies also had to be unembalmed, so those belonging to medical schools weren't suitable for Hyatt's purposes.

Hyatt had a solution. In 1951, he and his colleagues set up a body-donation program. They didn't limit themselves to bones. They removed many types of tissue, including fascia, veins, skin, and corneas. They also opened a special operating suite to harvest the tissue. By the end of that year, the Naval Tissue Bank had procured tissue from fifteen cadavers. Soon they were supplying tissue to civilian hospitals.

Hyatt offered the tissue free of charge. In return, he asked only that the surgeons report back with their results. With their input, Dr. Hyatt and his colleagues at the tissue bank constantly refined their approach. Between 1950 and 1980, they pioneered methods—none of which Hyatt bothered to patent—for disinfecting tissue, for freeze-drying it so that it would last longer in transit, and for screening donors for disease.

The Navy tissue bank soon gave rise to other tissue banks. Many hospitals established their own bone banks. If a surgeon needed bone to repair a joint, for example, he simply went to the freezer, removed a piece of bone, and ground it up or shaped it with his scalpel into the size he needed for a given operation. Many hospitals with burn centers also set up their own skin banks for treating burn victims.

When the U.S. Navy Tissue Bank finally closed, others took its place. During the 1980s, nonprofit community tissue banks began popping up all around the country. Tissue-bank employees approached the families of people who had died in local hospitals about tissue donation and then made the donated tissue available to local doctors.

As the amount of available tissue grew, so did its uses. Surgeons routinely used cadaver ligaments and tendons to treat sports injuries. They discovered they could use cadaver menisci to replace torn menisci in the living. They cut cadaver tibia into new shapes to replace herniated discs in the spine. They ground up cadaver bones into chips to help rebuild fractured jaws and to support dental implants.

Soon, for-profit companies joined the fray. Entrepreneurs saw the growing demand for tissue. They also saw that none of the basic techniques of the field had been patented. They set themselves up as "processors," middlemen who bought tissue from the nonprofits and cleaned it. Each company used a different process to rid the tissue of bacteria, many of which they copied directly from Hyatt. Some used gamma radiation. Some used antibiotics or disinfectant cocktails. Then they packaged the tissue and distributed it to hospitals. In 1984, CryoLife became the first big processing company on the scene. Osteotech followed in 1986. Both are now very profitable companies.

By the early 1990s, tissue banking was becoming an

industry. Profit-driven processors patented their cleansing cocktails and created "product lines" from human bone, transforming it into highly lucrative, ready-made products like bone paste and screws, chips, and dowels. They wrapped these ready-made products in glossy packaging and marketed them to hospitals just as they would any other medical device.

Still, there was no oversight by the U.S. government. Without regulation, some companies did as they pleased, cutting corners on safety to increase their profits. By the time Brian Lykins died, CryoLife had stopped culturing its tissue before immersing it in an antibiotic rinse. Pretesting is an important step in tissue processing. A company like Cryo-Life, which used a special antibiotic rinse, needed to establish the amount of bacteria on the tissue before it could decide how to treat it. What's more, the rinse could have created false negatives; if there had been bacteria on it at some point, the company might not have known. A 1997 memo from the company's quality-assurance officer suggested the company stop the testing step as a cost-saving measure.

It took the death of Brian Lykins to bring about real change. In May 2003, Senator Susan Collins of Maine held a senate hearing demanding that the FDA finalize regulations that it had proposed years before to ensure tissue safety.

In 1993, the FDA issued an interim rule, implemented five years later, which required tissue banks to screen donors for risk factors and to test their tissue for HIV, hepatitis, and certain communicable diseases. Finally, in 2004, the agency also began to require tissue banks to report deviations in manufacturing and to follow specific safety practices.

Still, no one has proposed legislation that goes beyond the monitoring of tissue safety. There has been no movement toward regulating the business as a whole. The Uniform Anatomical Gift Act of 1987 prohibits the buying and selling of tissue, but this law is not enforced. Unlike organ-procurement groups, tissue banks are not required to be nonprofits. No one audits their finances. And although tissue banks receive donations from the public, they still aren't required to disclose anything to donors.

Current regulations don't address conflicts of interest, either. There's nothing preventing a funeral director or the owner of a crematorium, like Michael Brown, from opening his own transplant tissue bank and soliciting bodies from grieving families so he can sell the tissue for cold, hard cash. Competition for bodies has led tissue companies to collaborate with funeral directors and brokers from the underground trade. Together, they are funneling bodies into the transplant pipeline, an endeavor with far more dangerous consequences than that of someone like Michael Brown.

———

One day, I called up a funeral director I know named A. Gray Budelman. "I've got to talk to you," he said as soon as he heard my voice.

Budelman and I were friendly in the funny way that a reporter is friendly with a good source. I had interviewed him once about the funeral business, and finding him to be an engaging conversationalist, I called him every so often to chat.

Budelman has a history in the cadaver trade. In the 1980s, he transported surplus corpses from a medical school in North Carolina to other medical schools in the Northeast. "I used to bring them up driving. A hundred at a time," he told me. "I used a tractor-trailer." Budelman knew John Vincent Scalia—"Johnny," as he called him. He also knew Richard Santore, but unlike Santore, he had never threatened to strangle me.

But Budelman did like to shock me. Once, when I visited him in his wood-paneled New Jersey office, I found him sitting at his desk, poring over the obituaries. "These are my financial pages," he explained.

"Really?" I asked.

"Are you kidding?" he said. "It's a very competitive business. Why do you think funeral directors join the Masons and the Lions? It's so they can get all the people when they die." In a business where most people in the know also keep their mouth shut, Budelman liked to talk. And this was one of the many reasons I liked him.

Budelman wanted to chat today.

"So, what's up?" I asked him.

"A doctor came to see me the other day about procuring some bones."

A doctor? I thought. *Why would a doctor go looking for bones in a funeral home?* Like skin, heart valves, veins, arteries, and ligaments, bones are used for transplantation into living people. Like other transplant tissue, they are supposed to be procured in sterile settings, places like hospital operating rooms or surgical suites.

"What's his story?" I asked Budelman.

"Meet me at Pals Cabin," Budelman said.

Pals Cabin is a favorite lunch spot in West Orange, New Jersey. The restaurant has been around since the 1930s and still serves the same old-fashioned fare: lunch dishes like its hot roast beef sandwich, which Budelman likes to dip in warm beef juice. Inside, the restaurant resembles a ski lodge, with paneled walls and heavy wooden beams. The booths are comfortably wide, the waitresses are indifferent, and the lighting is dim, all of which make Pals Cabin an excellent place to carry on a conversation if you don't want to be seen or overheard. At the front, a long bar pumps out strong cocktails to politicians, dealmakers, doctors, lawyers, and the other regulars, like Budelman.

At noon one day the following week, Budelman met me in the Pals Cabin parking lot. "How's slime city?" he asked, gesturing with his head in the direction of New York and locking my hand in a tight grip.

"Fine, thanks," I replied.

He snickered.

Gray Budelman is a tall man with a closely cropped gray beard and blue eyes that are perpetually fixed on whatever happens to be in the distance. On his wrist he wears a gold bracelet that spells out G-R-A-Y, and on his pinkie, a diamond ring. He followed me inside the restaurant, where we settled into a booth.

Budelman wasted no time ordering a Jack Daniel's. "Twist of lemon and a dash of water," he instructed the waitress. While he sipped his cocktail, he told me about the visit from the doctor. "This character here is from Fort Lee, New Jersey," Budelman began, passing some papers across the table to me. One of the documents was a plain piece of paper, rather amateurish-looking, with a mission statement and a mysterious company profile for something called Biomedical Tissue Services: "Biomedical Tissue Services is dedicated to promoting and coordinating tissue donation while working with the highest ethical standards and quality professional services, through a commitment of excellence."

Budelman explained that the owner of Biomedical Tissue Services, a Dr. Michael Mastromarino, had stopped by his funeral home with a business proposition. Mastromarino wanted access to corpses, Budelman said, and the doctor asked him if he would be willing to approach families who came to him for funeral services about donating bones from the bodies of their loved ones. Mainly, Mastromarino was looking for arm bones and leg bones.

"I would get the family's go-ahead and authorize it, and they would send a technician out," Budelman explained. The technician would come to Budelman's funeral home in Orange, cut the bones from the corpse in his embalming room, and take them away.

"I don't know much about it," he went on, taking a long sip of his Jack Daniel's. "The guy gave me a brochure. We talked for a while. Most of the conversation, he was telling me about his other funeral directors who he was trying to explain it to and they didn't have a clue."

"What do they do with the bones?" I asked.

"They grind them up and they make shit," Budelman said impatiently. "I haven't got the foggiest idea. As I said, the fellow approached me, and I tried to figure out how I could work it the way I wanted to do things. That was all I cared about," he said. "It sounded like a pretty good deal."

I was reminded of something that Budelman once told me. "I'm like an old whore," he'd said. "I only get out of bed if there's money involved."

Apparently, the doctor did not disappoint in that respect. Mastromarino offered Budelman a flat fee for every donor he referred, ostensibly to cover the cost of using his back room for the procurement. This type of fee is what some people in the transplant business disparagingly call the "bounty."

When I asked Budelman how much he was offered, he gazed past me toward the woman in the next booth. His fingers drummed on the wood tabletop.

"Can you give me a ballpark range of what he would pay you?"

"Not really," he said.

"What amount would make you say yes to the deal?"

"Five hundred dollars and up," he replied.

"I just got to figure out how I can play it," Budelman said, producing a pack of wintergreen tobacco from his pocket. He wedged a fat pinch into his cheek and adjusted it for a while with his tongue. The best situation, he mused, would be one in which the body was going to be cremated.

That way he wouldn't have to do a lot of reconstruction to compensate for the missing bones.

"How did this guy find you?" I asked.

Budelman shrugged.

"Don't you want to know?" I said.

"No," he said, waving me away. "I get so many god-damn weirdos ringing my doorbell and calling me up every day that I don't pay much attention to them."

As I looked into it, I learned that Dr. Mastromarino, who lists himself as CEO of Biomedical Tissue Services, had been a dentist until a few years before. In November 2000, he surrendered his license after being arrested for possession of Demerol and a hypodermic needle and being under the influence of a controlled substance. So he set up an office in New York City, though he had no license, and in October 2002, New York authorities forced him out of practice.

By then, Mastromarino had teamed up with a funeral director to start Biotissue Technologies, now Biomedical Tissue Services Ltd. The funeral director, Joseph Nicelli, was a "trade embalmer" who worked on call, embalming bodies for different funeral homes in Brooklyn. Nicelli owned the embalming service, Regional Funeral Services, and the Brooklyn-based Daniel George Funeral Home. According to a report that Mastromarino filed with the New York State Department of Health, in 2003, Regional Funeral Services and a Harlem funeral home called New York Mortuary produced 230 bodies for Biomedical Tissue Services.

Like his counterparts in the body-parts trade, Mastromarino has tried to recruit medical-school dieners to supply him. In 2004, he approached the diener at Albert Einstein College of Medicine in the Bronx. "He said they wanted femurs," Vincent Ruggiero told me. "He said that they make screws out of them." When Ruggiero explained that the bodies had been donated to the school for education, not transplantation, and that they were embalmed, Mastromarino assured him that "freshness wasn't a big issue." Ruggiero said, "No way." But other dieners might very well have agreed.

———

Biomedical Tissue Services Ltd. was until recently part of a national network of tissue banks that supplies Regeneration Technologies, Inc., a for-profit processor in Florida. In 2003, the company, which is traded on the New York Stock Exchange, had $75 million in revenues.

Regeneration Technologies, Inc. grew out of a nonprofit tissue bank connected to the University of Florida. In 1998, when researchers at the tissue bank realized that some of the bone products they had developed could be very lucrative, they spun off the manufacturing arm of the business into Regeneration Technologies.

Like any manufacturer, a tissue processor depends on its raw materials for production. But in the tissue business, like the oil business, finding a consistent supplier is tough. RTI recognized this problem early on. When the company went public in 2000, it issued a caution to investors in the registration statement it filed with the SEC. "Due to seasonal changes in mortality rates, some scarce tissues that we use for our allografts are at times in particularly short supply. . . .

Any interruption of our business caused by the need to locate additional sources of tissue would significantly hurt our revenues, which could cause the market price of your shares to decline." This left the company in the awkward position of depending on a constant death rate for its continued success.

So RTI took a proactive approach. Brandishing its supersonic BioCleanse machine, which it presented as the gold standard in tissue-cleansing equipment, the company began buying up nonprofit tissue banks around the country, forming strategic alliances with others, and courting funeral directors like Gray Budelman. The tissue banks that RTI purchased became part of a new company, RTI Donor Services, which advertises itself as a nonprofit but is little more than a tissue funnel for the profitable RTI. This was a cozy setup and RTI knew it. The company rewarded its subsidiaries and their employees with stock options and bonuses for meeting their tissue quotas.*

In 1999, RTI paid $1.8 million for Georgia Tissue Bank, a community tissue bank in Atlanta. The previous year, it had funded another supplier, Allograft Resources in Wisconsin. Some employees at both tissue banks were given stock options. In 2000, RTI bought the Alabama Tissue Center, which specializes in heart valves, for close to $4 million in

---

* The compensation scheme laid out in its registration statement filed with the SEC included, among other things, a $100 bonus for RTI staff members who exceeded their tissue targets and $100 for every donor they obtained from a funeral home that exceeded the projected five funeral-home donors per month.

stock and cash. And in 2001, it took over New York Tissue Services, a tissue bank on Staten Island.

RTI even expanded overseas. As of this writing, it had distribution agreements in Germany, Austria, Switzerland, South Korea, Greece, Italy, Spain, and Portugal. The company also joined forces with Tutogen Medical, a tissue-processing company with offices in Germany. As part of the agreement, Tutogen would supply RTI with bone shafts from the legs of dead Europeans. Together, the two companies made plans to establish the University of Florida Tissue Bank Europe, now headquartered in Italy. Thanks in part to these and other scavenging activities, company revenues more than doubled between 1998 and 1999.

In the meantime, the company has been making inroads with the traditional gatekeepers of corpses: funeral directors. Other tissue banks avoid harvesting tissue in funeral homes for fear of contamination. But RTI has BioCleanse, which the company says eliminates any such risk. It has forged agreements with funeral homes in New York, Indiana, California, Arizona, and elsewhere. In New York, the funeral homes are known as "crystal partners."

To sell them on the idea, RTI flies funeral directors to Alachua, Florida, so they can see BioCleanse up close. The funeral directors always leave impressed. One man from California told me that as soon as a family signs up with his funeral home, he faxes their information to RTI—without telling the family. If the family later agrees to tissue donation, he gets a slice of the pie.

Like many newcomers to the business, RTI's CEO, Brian

Hutchison, came from the medical-device industry. He had been vice president of Worldwide Product Development and Distribution for Stryker, a $3.96 billion medical-equipment manufacturer. Stryker makes, among other things, orthopedic implants and bone substitutes.

I asked Hutchison what attracted him to the business. He explained that during his twelve years at Stryker, he had heard about the tissue business but was never very interested in it. "The industry was probably $200 million in revenue total. It wasn't very attractive," he said. Hutchison took notice, however, "when the industry grew from roughly $200 million to roughly $800 million from the early nineties to the late nineties." In December 2001, he became CEO of RTI. "At the end of the day, I view this as a manufacturer," he said.

As the tissue business has grown lucrative, medical-device companies have started to move in. It's a natural step for them. Their salespeople already have relationships with surgeons and hospitals, which makes them valuable partners for companies like RTI. "They have a sales force that gets out and gets to know their customers and wines and dines them and gives them the benefits. Free samples and that sort of thing," said Dr. Michael Strong, a pioneer at the Navy Tissue Bank. RTI's bone products, in turn, enable the device companies to expand their product lines.

The two sides of the trade in corpses have converged in corporate America. The same companies that buy body parts to showcase their devices are now distributing human tissue in glossy packaging. Medtronic buys spines from broker Arthur Rathburn to show off the company's new back-pain device. Medtronic also buys spinal bone products and paste from RTI, which it markets and distributes to hospitals and doctors around the country. Just as Medtronic recruits and rewards surgeons willing to test and promote surgical devices, they now recruit surgeons to try bone products made by RTI.

Brian Hutchison was also doing his part. Soon, he'd be meeting with a spine surgeon, "a key opinion leader." Unfortunately, Hutchison said, this particular surgeon was still using autograft bone—that is, bone taken from the patient's own body. "He still takes autograft bone and shapes it the way he wants it," Hutchison said in dismay, as though this method, long considered the gold standard by surgeons for certain procedures, was somehow misguided. Hutchison went on: "I asked him at a recent meeting, 'Why don't you believe in allograft?' And he said, 'I don't believe I can get a consistent supply and I don't believe I can get a safe supply and I don't believe I can get designs or products that can help in surgery.'"

Hutchison saw his chance. "I asked him, 'Would it be okay if I spent some time with you in surgery and watched you do this? In return, would you please come to RTI for a day and I'll pay for your flights and we'll teach you what the latest issues are with allograft? I'm not going to try and convert you. I want to learn and understand where the future of spine surgery is headed. The surgeon said, 'Okay.'"

RTI's subsidiary tissue banks get their raw materials by convincing donors and their families that there's a pressing need. They play on the generosity and altruism of the public to get donations. But their marketing efforts suggest that they're not simply meeting the current demand. In fact, they're also drumming up new business, increasing the demand so they can sell more "products," create an ever-more-pressing need for donated tissue, and boost their profits.

Several people who started out at the Navy Tissue Bank told me they were dismayed that companies had started profiteering on tissue. Dr. Michael Strong pointed out that the Navy offered its tissue for free. When he started, he said, it was about science. "In the past ten or fifteen years, it's become more of a trade. I have seen hospitals in which the sales guy comes in with a suitcase full of tissue and says, 'Here, try this largest bone block,' and scrubs into the operating room and they put it in and there's no record of that in the hospital." He added, "When you introduce the profit motive in this field, then the money drives decisions—and decisions are at the expense of safety."

———

Tissue selling is a secretive business. Today, more than 850,000 tissue transplants are performed every year, but the public understands very little about the process used to acquire and distribute the tissue. Most people assume that tissues, like organs, are lifesaving. They assume that because they have given tissue, it will, in turn, be given to a recipient. Few people are aware of the middlemen and the profit-making companies involved.

Tissue bankers see no reason to tell them. As a general rule, processors will not disclose tissue prices—Hutchison declined to comment on RTIs—nor will they reveal the amount of tissue that they obtain and sell every year; in some cases, processors will not even release specifics about where they acquire their tissue.

A common PR tactic is to portray such discussion as offensive to the memories of donors and to the feelings of donor families. Discussing such details could give donor families the wrong impression, tissue bankers say—it could make families feel as if their loved ones were nothing more than commodities.

But why is this? Donors to any other cause are entitled to know if their donation has been used to line someone's pockets. Whether they know it or not, donors are responsible for the profits of companies like RTI.

The FDA sides with the companies. The agency will not release any detailed information on the companies' products, their relationships with suppliers, or their processes. The agency has ruled that the amount of tissue a tissue bank sells, the names of its buyers, and its suppliers—is proprietary.

This cloak of secrecy affects even surgeons. A recent study of 340 hospitals around the country found that orthopedic surgeons, who may rely on tissue more than other surgeons, are surprisingly ignorant about the tissue business. Sixty-five percent of surgeons surveyed had no idea where the tissue they used came from or how it had been processed.

In 85 percent of the institutions surveyed, the employees ordering the tissue were not orthopedically trained. In most cases, they knew little to nothing about the practices of the tissue banks with which they placed their orders. Their main criterion for selecting their suppliers was how quickly and easily the companies could get them the parts they wanted. Cost was a second consideration. But methods of processing and retrieval were low on their list of criteria. Most of the surgeons thought that the tissue they were using was sterile, and in most cases it was not.

Surgeons don't always recognize problems as tissue-related. Patients who acquire bacterial infections through tissue, like Brian Lykins, often present nonspecific postoperative symptoms like nausea, fever, and redness around the surgical site. As Dr. Warren King, a California orthopedic surgeon, said, "If a patient has just had surgery and the knee is red hot and swollen anyway—is it red hot and swollen because you just had surgery or . . . because you have an infection there as well? It's not that easy to determine an infection in a knee post-op."

If surgeons don't recognize an infection, they can't report the problem to the tissue bank. It is then impossible for the tissue bank to warn other surgeons who may have used tissue from the same donor.

Even when doctors do recognize a problem, the tissue banks may be quick to dismiss it and reluctant to share information. Dr. King recalled one instance when one of his patients developed a bacterial infection in his knee that

King later learned had been contracted from the tissue. When King confronted the tissue bank, a tissue-bank official heatedly denied the charge. When King asked how the bank processed its tissues, the official said, "We can't tell you that. That's a proprietary secret."

"Am I going to compete with you?" King barked. "I don't have a tissue bank. I'm a physician trying to get the best for my patients and to protect my patients." King finally got some real answers—but only when his patient filed a lawsuit against the tissue bank.

From the moment I met Budelman, I wanted to see behind the veil of secrecy. Finally, in November 2003, after I had made several phone calls and sent two letters, RTI executives allowed me to visit the company's headquarters in Alachua, a town of 6,000 people just northwest of Gainesville, where the University of Florida is located.

Wendy Crites Wacker, a prim, cheerful blonde, met me at the front desk, where we began the company tour. Our first stop was the processing facility, a 65,000-square-foot building, where couriers deliver bones and other types of human tissue every day in coolers. The company will not release exact numbers, but CEO Brian Hutchison says RTI processes tissue from "fewer than 4,000" corpses every year. Federal regulations don't stipulate where tissue can be harvested. Some of it might be removed from a corpse in a morgue or a medical examiner's office. Some might come from a surgical suite in a local tissue bank or from the embalming room in a funeral home.

The manufacturing facility is a large warehouse. Sitting off to the side of the company's other buildings in a lush, green office park, it is constructed around a central area known as the "processing core." There tissue is transformed into products under sterile conditions.

I followed Wacker into the building, and we were met by a hum one would expect to hear in a factory. She informed me that we would not be able to enter the core or to see any of the action up close. "You can't walk in there unless you are suited up and gowned in and all of that kind of stuff," she explained, leading me along a wide hallway with a shiny floor. One wall featured a poster board with pictures of RTI's many products—the Cornerstone, the Tangent, and MD-II, and others, a variety of small anchors, chips, dowels, and wedges—the sort of implements one might see in a carpentry shop, but these were fashioned from pure white bone. "It's all precision-tooled," Wacker said proudly.

One of RTI's other star products is Regenafil, an injectable bone paste. I realized this must have been what Gray Budelman meant when he mentioned grinding up bone. One form of the paste contains tiny chunks of bone. Another contains larger pieces. Both contain a gelatin-carrier base made from pigs. "It's mostly like a filler, in layman's terms. To fill in the gaps," Wacker said. "If you have any holes in the jawbone, it actually grows new bone."

Like any manufacturing process, the manner in which human tissue becomes a product involves many steps. First, the coolers are dropped off at a receiving area. After they are logged in, the tissue is removed and placed in a quarantine freezer at −50°C. "It's nippy in there," Wacker said. Each cooler that arrives should contain a vial of the donor's blood, which is tested for HIV, hepatitis, and syphilis. If it clears these tests, the tissue is removed from the freezer and a technician cleans off any bits of flesh that still cling to it. Then it is repackaged and carried into another room, where it is cut and tooled into various shapes and sizes on a FADAL, a machine found in many factories.

An ingenious and versatile machine, the FADAL translates blueprints into computer code, which instructs the machine how to cut the material in question. It's the type of machine that Lockheed Martin and Boeing use to cut aluminum.

Wacker led me to a narrow window through which I could see a tall young man dressed in a white gown and mask. He was stooped over a sleek lab table, staring at a series of bone screws. Behind him, another man lowered the head of a FADAL machine onto a piece of bone, sending bits of white dust flying. "The reason that we use so much computer-controlled machinery is because there is such a thing as human error," Wacker said. "If we have a technician who makes a mistake on a piece of tissue, then it can't be used anymore. It's a disservice to the donor family."

After the tissue is cut, it goes into BioCleanse, RTI's patented cleansing system. BioCleanse resembles a state-of-the-art washing machine. It can scour and wash many different types of tissue, including bone. "The technician just shuts the door and presses a button. It takes out all the human error. It's all computer-controlled," Wacker said. BioCleanse can remove all blood, lipids, marrow, bacteria, fungi, and spores within five hours. It is also designed to remove HIV, hepatitis B, and hepatitis C, even though those viruses are screened for before the tissue enters BioCleanse. "It pulls them all out," Wacker gushed. "What you have left is a clean, white bone."

Everything was modern and nothing had been left to chance. Once the tissue is cleaned, Wacker explained, it may be freeze-dried, depending on the type. Then it is packaged and labeled and readied for shipping. "Every single piece of tissue is in a package that has a bar code sticker on it," Wacker said. "The sticker will tell where the tissue came from and relate it to medical records, and it will relate to the donor-procurement agency who procured it." In the shipping room, there were shelves with plastic bags full of bones waiting to be sent to distributors.

The tone of my tour was entirely upbeat, full of marvel at the wonders produced by computer-controlled equipment and cleansing procedures. It was easy to forget that human corpses were driving the gears of this process. As I followed Wacker around, I recalled something Augie Perna had said: "That torso that you're living in right now is just flesh and bones. To me, it's a product."

I wanted to see the machine that makes Regenafil bone paste, but Wacker forced a smile and said the machine was deep inside the core and off-limits to visitors. After our tour, she led me back to the main building and ushered me into a plush conference room to meet with RTI's CEO, Brian Hutchison. I sat down at a sleek table made of dark wood. Resting on the table was a narrow wooden case resembling a jewelry box. The box had been fitted with a glass lid through which I could see pieces of what appeared to be pure white bone.

As I gazed at the bone pieces, Brian Hutchison strolled in. In his early forties, Hutchison is tall and handsome. He wore a tailored gray woolen suit and exuded the confidence of a successful salesman. In 2003, Hutchison earned half a million dollars. As of this writing, his stock options were worth more than $4 million.

On the subject of donation, he was careful to be somber. "It's the last good thing your loved one can do."

———

Hutchison's words haunted me.

A year later, the Brooklyn District Attorney in New York launched a criminal investigation into one of RTI's suppliers. The target of the investigation was Biomedical Tissue Services, the tissue bank run by Michael Mastromarino, the ex-dentist who had approached Gray Budelman, looking for bones. According to those familiar with the investigation, the DA was looking into allegations that Dr. Mastromarino had been harvesting and stealing body parts from New York funeral homes and selling them to RTI and two other processors for as much as $7,000 each.

The details of the case were as familiar as they were chilling. Like Allen Tyler, Mastromarino performed his grisly work on metal gurneys in the embalming rooms of funeral homes. From a thousand or so dead subjects, Mastromarino lifted bones, tendons, skin, ligaments, and heart valves. When he was finished, he replaced the missing bones with plumber's polyvinyl chloride pipe, sewed the bodies up, and hauled them back to his tissue bank in Fort Lee, New Jersey. The DA is investigating whether Mastromarino, in fact, obtained consent from all of the families.

Later, Mastromarino packed the parts in ice and shipped them out via FedEx.

The business was reminiscent of Michael Brown's. But these body parts were not destined for hotel conference rooms or underground brokers. They were headed for hospitals, where they were to be transplanted into living people like Brian Lykins. In this case, Mastromarino was selling body parts under the watchful eyes of the FDA. In fact, the FDA had inspected his company, and the agency was well aware that he obtained parts from funeral homes. Their advice to him? Make sure the embalming rooms are kept clean.

Like Brown, Mastromarino was blessed with plenty of eager clients. According to those close to the investigation, Mastromarino had no trouble selling his deceitfully acquired wares. He simply provided his clients with forged consent forms and partial death certificates, the sources said. In one potentially dangerous case reported by the New York *Daily News*, the records of a woman who had died of drug abuse were changed to indicate death from cardiac arrest.

Many of the body parts harvested by Mastromarino wound up at Regeneration Technologies Inc. in the same facility that I had visited, where they were shuttled through factory machines, "tooled" into neat shapes, and reborn— thanks to BioCleanse—as pristine "products." As of this writing, it's not clear if the company ever questioned Mastromarino about the body parts he sold them, or if, like so many buyers in the morally ambiguous cadaver trade, they simply accepted what they were told. RTI, after all, actively encourages its suppliers to access bodies through funeral homes. In 2004, the company had relationships with as many as 300 funeral homes around the country.

With each passing day, the investigation grew. Soon, police were investigating at least six funeral homes in New York and several more in Pennsylvania, New Jersey, and Florida.

Meanwhile, it was business as usual in the cadaver trade. While detectives from New York's major case squad were busy chasing down new leads, RTI was busy reassuring stockholders. In a press release, CEO Brian Hutchison promised investors that "RTI takes every precaution available to ensure the safety of the patients receiving its processed tissue." Yet after the scandal broke, the company took a full week to announce a recall of products made with what might have been stolen tissue.

One Saturday night, as I flipped through stories about Mastromarino in the local papers, the phone rang. It had been four years since another phone call with an anatomist first alerted me to the existence of the underground cadaver trade.

"This thing has only begun," a deep voice said. "The tentacles reach to many different places. One doesn't know where it's going to stop."

Yes, I thought. *Soon, the interwoven tentacles of the body brokers would emerge once again, somewhere new.*

Acknowledgments

I interviewed hundreds of people for this book: the families of deceased victims, detectives, brokers, and curiosity seekers. The families deserve special thanks for sharing their often painful stories with me, among them, Mike DiMeglio (who spoke so eloquently of his stepfather Ronald King); Ruth Storr; Paul, Joyce, and Joy Zamazanuk; June Reynolds; Allan Shull; and Jane Shull.

I am grateful to Dr. Todd Olson and Ronn Wade for the countless hours they spent teaching me about anatomical education and to Detective Rene Rodriguez, who was always generous with his time.

This book would have never come into being had it not been for my wonderful agent, David Halpern at the Robbins Office, who recognized the potential in the story from the very first lead, found a home for it at *Harper's* magazine, and encouraged me to turn the article into a book. Throughout the entire process, he has given me his unwavering encouragement and support and I am grateful to have him by my side.

If it hadn't been for Ed Shanahan, a former editor at *My Generation* magazine, I would have never fallen on this topic. Sometimes it takes just one question to uncover an important story and Ed had the sense to ask it.

I owe an enormous debt to Luke Mitchell, my brilliant editor at *Harper's*, who gave me the time I needed to investigate the story wherever it led me, from the suburbs of New Jersey to the beaches of Miami, and whose enthusiasm for the topic of corpses never ceased. His high standards inspired me to do my absolute best work, and, without his editorial guidance, I could have never produced an award-winning article.

My lasting gratitude goes to Charlie Conrad at Broadway Books for believing in my idea and leading the way. Becky Cole and Alison Presley at Broadway contributed invaluable insights during the editing process, and Amelia Zalcman gave me wise counsel. Finally, Joanna Pinsker and David Drake—you are wizards.

A special thanks goes to Andrew Szanton, who was there, day or night, always ready with the right words of encouragement and to Michele Comandini, who combed the manuscript for errors. Any errors that exist in the text are entirely my own.

Finally, I am grateful to my family and friends, especially my parents, Richard and Virginia Cheney, and my brother Ben Cheney and his girl-friend Jiwon Lee, who have put up with endless gory discussions about body parts and corpse brokers, who encouraged me to keep going, and who were always understanding when deadlines meant that I could not spend more time with them.

Above all, I wish to thank my soon-to-be husband, Benjamin Bailes, who patiently read the manuscript in its many incarnations and whose contributions improved it immeasurably. He is a fine editor, a tireless cheerleader, and a wonderful friend. Thank you for standing fast beside me and making it all worthwhile.

Notes

The following notes list the most important sources for each chapter. They do not include the source of every fact or quotation in the book. Quotes that are not cited came from interviews I conducted during my research.

Introduction

My main source for the introduction was a visit to the Trump International Sonesta Beach Resort. I relied on an interview with Marsha Newton, from the Office of Clinical Standards and Quality at the Centers for Medicare and Medicaid for information about organ-procurement organizations. I also drew on an interview with UNOS spokesperson Anne Paschke. The National Organ Transplant Act of 1984 and the Uniform Anatomical Gift Acts of 1968 and 1987 provided additional information. The history of funerals was based on *Inventing the American Way of Death, 1830–1920*, by James J. Farrell. Cremation statistics were provided by CANA (Cremation Association of North America). The tens of thousands of bodies that enter the cadaver trade includes those that are processed for tissue transplantation and those used for education and research.

1. Wilderness

My main source for this chapter was Jim Farrelly's mother, Joyce Zamazanuk. Interviews with Jim's sister, Joy, his stepfather, Paul, and his long-time partner, Billy Baker, provided additional information.

My main sources for the prevalence of body-parts thefts during autopsies were the following court cases: *Brotherton vs. Cleveland et al.* and *Whaley vs. County of Tuscola*. I also drew on reporting by Ralph Frammolino in the *Los Angeles Times*. In 1997, Frammolino revealed that the Los Angeles coroner was selling corneas removed during autopsies to the Doheny Eye and Tissue Transplant Bank for $215 to $335 per set. Many of the corneas were taken without explicit permission from their loved ones. I also drew on a State of New York Department of Health Investigation into the Onondaga county Medical Examiner's Office. The Onondaga Medical Examiner was found to have retained more than 100 body parts from autopsied bodies without permission during the 1980s. Articles about the Onondaga Medical Examiner case by John O'Brien in *The Post-Standard* between 1989 and 2002 provided further information. See also Chapter Six: Dr. Martin Spector bought body parts that had been harvested from autopsied bodies. Allegations of body-parts theft during autopsies have arisen most recently at the Medical Examiner's office in Portland, Maine, and at the Office of the Chief Medical Examiner in Boston.

For cases of body parts thefts in funeral homes, see Chapters 2, 3, and 7. Also, *People vs. Michael Francis Brown et al, People vs. David Sconce et al,* and *Bruno vs. English Bros. Funeral Home et al.*

2. An Ideal Situation and 3. The "Toolers"

My main source for these chapters was the Riverside County District Attorney's case file on Michael Francis Brown. I also relied heavily on transcripts from the criminal grand jury proceedings and from the proceedings of Brown's sentencing. Specifics about the case were provided by Riverside Sheriff's Investigator Rene Rodriguez, Investigator Robert Joseph, Sergeant Jeff Mullins, and Riverside District Attorney Karen Gorham.

Facts about David Sconce's crimes were drawn from three books: *Ashes: Terrifying True Horror of a Macabre Criminal Career,* by Joseph James, *A Family Business,* by Ken Englade, and *Chop Shop,* by Kathy Braidhill.

Descriptions of events in the history of Bio-Tech Anatomical and California Bio-Science were drawn from grand jury transcripts and interviews that I conducted with Michael Brown and his employees, associates, and acquaintances. Jennifer Bittner was a primary source of information. Louie Terrazas, John Schultz, and Kathy Gross helped fill out the story. Interviews with Rose Tyler, Allen Tyler's wife, and Kenneth Carter, Tyler's best friend, provided additional information.

For information about Ronald King, I relied on an interview with King's stepson, Mike DiMeglio. For the description of King's dismemberment, I referred to documents from Brown's case file and an interview with Jennifer Bittner and with Allen Tyler.

4. "As Soon as You Die, You're Mine"

My main sources for this chapter were interviews with Agostino Perna, Allen Tyler, Mike Charloff, and Dave Myers. Dr. Harry Reich and Dr. Earl

Sands provided additional information about advancements in minimally invasive surgery.

I also relied heavily on observations that I made during a visit to the IMET conference at the Trump International Sonesta Beach Resort in 2003.

For background on ScienceCare Anatomical, I referred to a letter from James E. Rogers to Michael Francis Brown obtained from the California Department of Health Services. I also drew on information obtained during interviews with Michael Brown, Agostino Perna, and James E. Rogers. For information about ScienceCare's customers, I relied on requests made by surgical-equipment companies and doctors to the Anatomical Board of the State of Florida.

Information about the conferences held in Florida was taken from requests to import body parts filed with the Anatomical Board of the State of Florida between 1993 and 2003. I also relied on several interviews with the executive director of the Anatomical Board, Dr. Lynn Romrell.

My sources for the section about Richard Santore were a New York State Department of Health Case Report filed in 1987; an Associated Press report on May 3, 1979, "The Crazy Eddie of the Cremation Business," which appeared in *New York City Business* (now *Crain's New York Business*) June 3, 1985; and an interview with Richard Santore.

For my description of the bloody FedEx boxes, I relied on an investigative report filed by the Kirkwood Police on November 5, 2003, and articles published in the *St. Louis Dispatch* on November 20, November 23, and December 11, 2003, by Todd C. Frankel. An interview with Mike Nimoff of Airways Freight Corp. provided information about the company's work with body brokers.

Information about the surgical training centers of specific companies such as Medtronic was taken from company Web sites, interviews, and documents filed with the SEC.

5. The Resurrection Men

My main sources for this chapter were *A History of Surgery,* by Roger Ellis, *The Diary of a Resurrectionist 1811–1812: To Which Are Added an Account of the Resurrection Men in London and a Short History of the Passing of the Anatomy Act,* by James Blake Bailey, *A Traffic of Dead Bodies: Anatomy and Embodied Social Identity in Nineteenth-Century America,* by Michael Sappol, *Bones in the Basement: Postmortem Racism in Nineteenth-Century Medical Training,* by Robert L. Blakely and Judith M. Harrington, and *The Life of Sir Astley Cooper,* by Bransby Cooper. *The Regency Underworld,* by Donald Low, was another great resource.

Two journal articles were essential to my reporting: *The Journal of*

Medical Education, volume 37, 1962, "Medical Education from the Ground Up or Our Late Resurrection Men," by Sam L. Clark, and *Michigan History*, LV/1, 1971, "Body Snatching in the Midwest," by Martin Kaufman and Leslie L. Hanawalt. The Michigan anatomist's quote on page 117 was taken from this article.

I also relied on articles about body snatching that appeared throughout 1878 in the *New York Times*.

For information about the passage of poor laws in the United States, I referred to the "Report of the Select Committee of the House of Representatives on So Much of the Governor's Speech at the June Session, 1830, as Relates to Legalizing the Study of Anatomy."

My main sources for the section about changes in medical school enrollment and the demand for cadavers were David Blumenthal's article "New Steam from an Old Cauldron," which appeared in *The New England Journal of Medicine*, volume 350(17), April 2004; an interview with Dr. Todd Olson, professor of anatomy at the Albert Einstein College of Medicine; and an interview with Michelle Johnson, founder of MCJ Consulting.

6. "Brokered Sounds Bad, Doesn't It?"

For the section on Dr. Martin Spector, I relied on interviews with Dr. Richard Greathouse, Detective Daniel Rosenstein, and Pennsylvania Supreme Court Justice Ronald Castille, formerly a Philadelphia District Attorney. Court documents from the *Commonwealth of Pennsylvania v. Martin Spector*, specifically court testimony from Detective Francis Coward, provided additional information.

I also relied on coverage of the Spector case by reporters at the *Philadelphia Inquirer* and the *Philadelphia Daily News*.

My main sources for the section on Arthur Rathbun were interviews with current and former University of Michigan Medical School employees. Rathbun's lawsuit against the Board of Regents of the University of Michigan was filed in the State of Michigan in the Circuit Court for the County of Washtenaw, September 26, 1991.

Details of International Biological's business activities were taken from documents filed by the company with the New York State Department of Health, the State of Florida Anatomical Board, and Anatomy Department records at the State University of New York Upstate Medical School in Syracuse.

My main sources for the section on Allen Tyler were UTMB Anatomy Department records from 1998 to 2001 and an interview with FBI agent

Jim Walsh, who was in charge of the Tyler investigation. An interview with Allen Tyler before his death, and interviews with Rose Tyler and Kenneth Carter, provided additional information.

I also relied on coverage of the UTMB case by Kenneth Moran in the *Houston Chronicle,* and Katy Vine, whose article "Little Shop of Horrors" appeared in the *Texas Monthly* in August 2003.

For the material on the UCLA Medical School willed-body scandals, I relied on coverage by the *Los Angeles Times.* I also used documents from a Department of Health Services investigation into Ernest Nelson's business. For Henry Reid's financial background, I relied on 1999 US Bankruptcy Court Documents from the Central District of California.

My main source for UCLA's legal argument was the Regents of the University of California's Brief Re Preliminary Pleading Issues in *Beatrice Cohen, Joyce Maddox, John Faraday v. Johnson & Johnson et al.*

For a history of Tulane, I referred to the *History of Medical Education in New Orleans from Its Birth to the Civil War,* by A. E. Fossier, M.D. The section about Tulane and the Army was drawn from interviews with Dr. Gerald Kirby, Fran Simon of Tulane University, and June Reynolds, Jane Shull, and Allan Shull, Charley Reynolds's relatives. Interviews with Steve Rountree, Chuck Dasey, and Lieutenant Colonel Roman Hayda of the U.S. Army provided additional information. I also referred to a contract between the U.S. Army and National Anatomical Service and a letter from Dr. Mary Bitner Anderson to Mrs. June Reynolds, May 17, 2004.

Many news reports were also helpful. Most important was a series of articles about Tulane and the U.S. Army by Stewart Yerton in the *Times-Picayune,* an article by Heidi Singer in the *New York Post* on March 12, and a BBC report on March 11, 2004.

For information about Louisiana State University Health Sciences Center in Shreveport, I relied on interviews with Dr. Leonard Seelig and Janie Binderim, as well as LSU Shreveport Anatomy Department documents.

Observations about the AACA were taken from my visit to the AACA Conference in Moraga, California, in June 2004 and interviews with Dr. Donald Cahill, formerly chairman of the Anatomy Department at the Mayo School of Medicine; Dr. Todd Olson, professor of anatomy at the Albert Einstein College of Medicine; Dr. Lawrence Ross, adjunct professor, Department of Neurobiology and Anatomy, University of Texas–Houston Medical School; and Ronn Wade, director of the Anatomy Board of Maryland. Information about the Johnson & Johnson companies was obtained via e-mail from spokespersons Sarah Colamarino and Jeff Lebaw.

7. The Bone Machine

Some of the information about Brian Lykins was drawn from testimony by his father and mother, Steve and Leslie Lykins, at the U.S. Senate Hearing, "Tissue Banks: The Dangers of Tainted Tissues and the Need for Federal Regulation," May 14, 2003. I also relied heavily on court documents from the case *Lykins v. CryoLife* and reporting by Sandra Blakeslee for the *New York Times*. Interviews with CDC epidemiologist Dr. Marion Kainer, Minnesota Department of Health epidemiologist Dr. Henry Hull, and Minnesota epidemic intelligence officer Dr. Mei Castor provided additional information.

My main sources for Bonny Gonyer's story were interviews with Bonny Gonyer and court documents from *Gonyer v. CryoLife*. I also drew on FDA inspection reports of CryoLife and morbidity and mortality reports from the Centers for Disease Control, specifically "Update: Allograft—Associated Bacterial Infections," on March 15, 2002, and "Invasive Streptoccus Pyrogenes After Allograft implantation," on December 5, 2003.

Dr. Warren King and Dr. Scott Barbour's article, "Basic Science Update. The Safe and Effective Use of Allograft Tissue—An Update," which appeared in *The American Journal of Sports Medicine* in 2003, provided information about the challenges surgeons face in detecting bacterial infections from allograft. I also drew on an interview with Dr. King. The study of surgeons and their knowledge of human tissue appeared in 2004 in the *Journal of Arthroplasty*.

My main sources for the history of tissue banking were interviews with Dr. Michael Strong, Dr. Theodore Malinin, Dr. Gary E. Friedlander, and Jeffrey Prottas. "The US Navy Tissue Bank: 50 Years on the Cutting Edge," by Dr. Michael Strong, and *Transplanting Human Tissue: Ethics, Policy and Practice,* edited by Stuart J. Youngner, Martha W. Anderson, and Renie Schapiro, provided additional information. Specifics on RTI's compensation scheme were taken from the latter book.

My main sources for the section about Michael Mastromarino were interviews with A. Gray Budelman and annual reports filed by Mastromarino on behalf of his company, Biomedical Tissue Services, with the New York State Department of Health. My sources for information about Mastromarino's dental license were the New York State Education Department and the New Jersey State Board of Dentistry. Articles written by William Sherman in the *Daily News* provided information on the DA's investigation into Mastromarino and Nicelli.

For the section about Regeneration Technologies, Inc., I relied on a visit to RTI headquarters in November 2003, SEC documents filed by the company, FDA inspection reports of RTI and Southeast Tissue Alliance, and a transcript from the 2001 Senate Hearing, "Tissue Banks: Is the Federal Government's Oversight Adequate?," May 2001.

Bibliography

Anderson, Martha W., Renie Schapiro, and Stuart J. Youngner, eds. *Transplanting Human Tissue: Ethics, Policy and Practice*. New York: Oxford University Press, 2004.

Bailey, James Blake. *The Diary of a Resurrectionist 1811–1812: To Which Are Added an Account of the Resurrection Men in London and a Short History of the Passing of the Anatomy Act*. London: Swan Sonnenschein, 1896.

Ball, James Moore. *The Sack-'Em-Up Men: An Account of the Rise and Fall of the Modern Resurrectionists*. Edinburgh: Oliver and Boyd, 1928.

Blakely, Robert L., and Judith M. Harrington, eds. *Bones in the Basement: Postmortem Racism in Nineteenth-Century Medical Training*. New York: Smithsonian Books, 1997.

Braidhill, Kathy. *Chop Shop*. New York: Pinnacle Books, 1993.

Cahill, Donald R., and Sandy C. Marks, Jr. "Memorandum Adopted by the American Association of Clinical Anatomists—May 31, 1999." *Clinical Anatomy*, vol. 4, 1991.

Campbell, Ronald, William Heisel, and Mark Katches. "The Body Brokers." *The Orange County Register*, April 2000.

Clark, Sam L. "Medical Education from the Ground Up, or Our Late Resurrection Men." *The Journal of Medical Education*, vol. 37, 1962.

Cooper, Bransby Blake. *The Life of Sir Astley Cooper, Bart. Interspersed with Sketches from his Note-Books of Distinguished Contemporary Characters*. London: John W. Parker, West Strand, 1843.

Englade, Ken. *A Family Business*. New York: St. Martin's Press, 1992.

Farrell, James J. *Inventing the American Way of Death, 1830–1920.* Philadelphia: Temple University Press, 1980.

Fido, Martin. *Body Snatchers: A History of the Resurrectionists 1742–1832.* London: Weidenfeld and Nicolson, 1988.

Hanawalt, Leslie L., and Martin Kaufman. "Body Snatching in the Midwest." *Michigan History*, vol. 1, 1971.

Hearing before the Subcommittee on Investigations of the Committee on Governmental Affairs US Senate. "Tissue Banks: Is the Federal Government's Oversight Adequate?" May 2001.

———— "Tissue Banks: The Dangers of Tainted Tissues and the Need for Federal Regulation," May 2003.

Heaton, Claude. "Body Snatching in New York City." *New York State Journal of Medicine*, vol. 43, 1943.

Hedges, Stephen J., and William Gaines. "Donor Bodies Milled into Growing Profits: Little Regulated Industry Thrives on Unsuspecting Families." *Chicago Tribune*, May 21, 2000.

Hopkinson, Francis. *An Oration Which Might Have Been Delivered to the Students in Anatomy.* Philadelphia, 1789.

Iserson, Kenneth V. *Death to Dust: What Happens to Dead Bodies?* Tucson: Galen Press, 1994.

James, Joseph. *Ashes: Terrifying True Horror of a Macabre Criminal Career.* New York: Berkley Publishing Group, 1994.

Ladenheim, Jules Calvin. "The Doctor's Mob of 1788." *Journal of the History of Medicine,* Winter 1950.

Low, Donald A. *The Regency Underworld.* London: J.M. Dent & Sons Ltd., 1982.

Lavernia, Carlos, M.D., Malinin, Theodore, M.D., Temple, Thomas, M.D., and Carlos Moreya, M.D. "Bone and Tissue Allograft Use by Orthopaedic Surgeons." *The Journal of Arthroplasty,* vol. 19, no. 4, 2004.

Mahoney, Julia D. "The Market for Human Tissue." *Virginia Law Review*, March 2002.

Mott, Valentine. "An Address Introductory to a Course of Lectures at the College of Physicians and Surgeons." New York: Joseph H. Jennings, 1850.

Office of the Inspector General. "Oversight of Tissue Banking," January 2001.

————. "Informed Consent in Tissue Donation: Expectations and Realities," January 2001.

Report of the Select Committee of the House of Representatives on So Much of the Governor's Speech at the June Session, 1830, as Relates to

Legalizing the Study of Anatomy. Boston: Dutton and Wentworth, 1831.

Richardson, Ruth. *Death, Dissection and the Destitute.* London: Routledge & Kegan Paul Ltd., 1987.

Sappol, Michael. *A Traffic of Dead Bodies: Anatomy and Embodied Social Identity in Nineteenth Century America.* Princeton: Princeton University Press, 2002.

Strong, Michael. "The US Navy Tissue Bank: 50 Years on the Cutting Edge." *Cell and Tissue Banking,* vol. 1, 2000.

About the Author

ANNIE CHENEY's magazine work has appeared in *Harper's* and *My Generation*. Her *Harper's* article that is the basis of this book was awarded the 2005 Deadline Club Award for Best Feature Reporting by the Society of Professional Journalists. She has also contributed stories to numerous public radio shows, including NPR's *All Things Considered*. She lives in New York City.